JUNIOR
READING EXPERT

A Theme-Based Read... EFL Learners

Level **2**

JUNIOR
READING EXPERT

Level 2

Series Editor	Ji-hyun Kim
Project Editors	Eun-kyung Kim, Jun-hee Kim, Yoon-joung Choi
Contributing Writers	Curtis Thompson, Bryce Olk, Angela Hai Yue Lan, Patrick Ferraro, MyAn Le, Keeran Murphy
Illustrators	Soo-hyeon Lee, Yoon-seo Jung, Seol-hui Kim
Design	Hoon-jung Ahn, Ji-young Ki
Editorial Designer	Sun-hee Kim

ISBN	979-11-253-4041-6 53740
Photo Credits	www.shutterstock.com

INTRODUCTION

Junior Reading Expert is a four-level reading course for EFL readers, with special relevance for older elementary school students and junior high school students. Students will acquire not only reading skills but also knowledge of various contemporary and academic topics.

Features

Covers Dynamic, Contemporary Topics

Engaging topics, including culture, sports, and literature, are developed in an easy and interesting way to motivate students.

Expands Knowledge

Each unit is composed of two closely related readings under one topic heading. These readings allow students to explore the theme in depth.

Features Longer Passages

EFL students are seldom exposed to long reading passages and therefore tend to find them difficult. Compelling and well-developed passages designed specifically for EFL students will help them learn to handle longer passages with ease.

Presents Different Text Types of Passages

Reading passages are presented as articles, letters, debates, interviews, and novels. This helps students become familiarized with a variety of writing formats and styles through different genres of readings.

Provides Various Exercises for Reading Skills

All readings are accompanied by different types of tasks, such as multiple choice, matching, short answer, true/false, and fill-in-the-blank. These exercises are carefully designed to develop the following reading skills: understanding main ideas, identifying details, drawing inferences, and recognizing organizational structures.

Series Overview

Each level of *Junior Reading Expert* is composed of 20 units, with two related readings accompanying each unit. The number of words in each Reading 1 passage is as follows:

Level 1: 150–170 words
Level 2: 170–190 words
Level 3: 190–210 words
Level 4: 210–230 words

Format

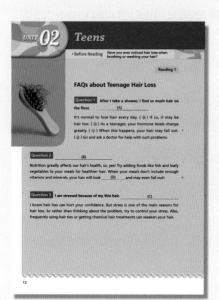

Reading 1

Reading 1 takes students into the first of the unit's two readings. Being the main reading of the unit, Reading 1 deals with various interesting and important topics in great depth. The passages gradually increase in difficulty as students progress through the book.

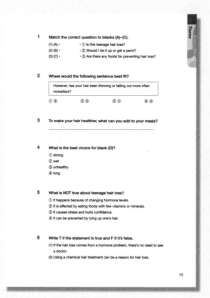

Different Types of Questions

A full page of different types of questions follows Reading 1. The questions concentrate on important reading skills, such as understanding the main idea, identifying details, drawing inferences, and recognizing the organizational structure.

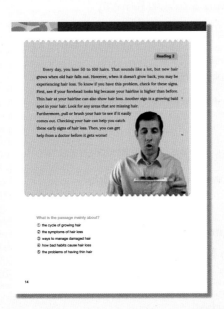

Reading 2

Reading 2 offers a second reading passage on the unit topic, the length of which is from 90 to 110 words. Reading 2 supplements Reading 1 with additional information, further explanation, or a new point of view.

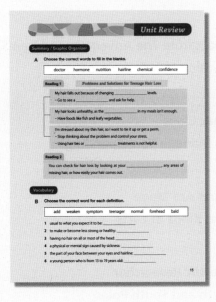

Unit Review

A Summary / Graphic Organizer
Either a summary or a graphic organizer is provided for Reading 1 and Reading 2 to facilitate a better understanding of the flow of passages. Performing this task also encourages the development of systematic comprehension skills.

B Vocabulary
Each unit is concluded with vocabulary practice. It checks students' knowledge of essential vocabulary words. Vocabulary practice requires students to either match definitions or choose words in context.

Table of Contents

Reading 1

Dear Mom and Dad,

I am traveling on the Trans-Siberian Railway. It is the longest train system in the world. It has several routes, but I'm riding on the line that goes from Moscow to Vladivostok. The journey is about 9,300 kilometers long and takes eight 5 days—that means I am covering about one-fourth of the earth from west to east!

Today is the sixth day of my journey. Being on the train never gets boring. ⓐ Most of the passengers are from Russia or China. ⓑ We share our food and enjoy the beautiful views 10 together. ⓒ It took many years to build the railway. ⓓ At night we sleep in our little beds.

For days we traveled through Siberia. Two days ago I got off the train to visit Lake Baikal. Known as the "Blue Eye of Siberia," it is the deepest and largest freshwater lake in the world. When I first saw it, I didn't know what to say. It was so huge and 15 beautiful! I ate a picnic lunch there and swam in the cold, blue water.

I can't wait to explore Vladivostok. From there, I will take a ferry to Japan.

Love,
Daniel

1   **What is Daniel's letter mainly about?**

① the beautiful nature of Russia

② visiting famous Russian cities

③ traveling on the Trans-Siberian train

④ the history of the Trans-Siberian Railway

2   **Which sentence is NOT needed in the passage?**

① ⓐ   ② ⓑ   ③ ⓒ   ④ ⓓ

3   **Which best describes Daniel's feelings in the 3rd paragraph?**

① bored

② proud

③ nervous

④ amazed

4   **What is suggested about the Trans-Siberian Railway?**

① It is the world's oldest railway system.

② One of its routes covers about 9,300 kilometers.

③ It helps travelers save a lot of time.

④ Passengers can order Russian and Chinese food on it.

5   **What is NOT mentioned about Daniel in the passage?**

① how long his train ride will take

② what he does on the train

③ what the purpose of his trip is

④ where he had a stopover

6   **Write T if the statement is true and F if it's false.**

(1) Daniel feels a little bored while traveling on the train.

(2) People cannot swim in Lake Baikal because it's too deep.

(3) Daniel will go to Japan after traveling to Vladivostok.

Experience Russia with a Trans-Siberian Railway Tour!

Tour Time: 11 days (all year)
Group Size: 10-15 people
Price per Person: $1,800

Schedule	
Day 1	Arrive in Moscow: A group meeting at the hotel
Day 2	Moscow: Free day in Moscow
Day 3-5	On train: Moscow to Irkutsk
Day 6	Arrive at Lake Baikal for 2 nights
Day 7	Free day at Lake Baikal
Day 8-10	On train: Irkutsk to Vladivostok
Day 11	Arrive in Vladivostok

What's Included	What's Not Included
· English-speaking tour guide · Accommodation in hotels with breakfast · 2nd-class train ticket	· Travel insurance · Russian visa

For booking and more information, please send an email to
sally@fabrussiantour.com or call **012-555-6789**.

What is NOT true about the Trans-Siberian Railway Tour?

① It takes more than a week.

② At least ten people will be on the tour.

③ Only one day will be used as a free day.

④ A train ticket and a tour guide service are provided.

⑤ Personal travel insurance and a Russian visa are not provided.

Summary / Graphic Organizer

A Choose the correct words to fill in the blanks.

ferry	longest	ride	swam	one-fourth

Reading 1

Daniel's Trip

The Trans-Siberian Railway

• It's the _____ train system in the world.

• One of its routes covers about _____ of the earth.

Daniel's Journey

• He is traveling from Moscow to Vladivostok.

• He is enjoying the beautiful scenery with other passengers.

• He visited Lake Baikal and _____ in the lake.

• After traveling to Vladivostok, he will go to Japan by _____.

Vocabulary

B Choose the correct word for each definition.

lake	view	accommodation	passenger	journey	include	huge

1 a place to stay or live: _____

2 what you can see from somewhere: _____

3 the act of traveling from one place to another: _____

4 someone who rides in a car, train, plane, or ship: _____

5 to have as a part of something else: _____

6 very large in size or amount: _____

Reading 1

FAQs about Teenage Hair Loss

Question 1   **After I take a shower, I find so much hair on the floor. _____(A)_____**

It's normal to lose hair every day. (ⓐ) If so, it may be hair loss. (ⓑ) As a teenager, your hormone levels change greatly. (ⓒ) When this happens, your hair may fall out. ₅ (ⓓ) Go and ask a doctor for help with such problems.

Question 2   _____(B)_____

Nutrition greatly affects our hair's health, so, yes! Try adding foods like fish and leafy vegetables to your meals for healthier hair. When your meals don't include enough vitamins and minerals, your hair will look _____(D)_____ and may even fall out! ₁₀

Question 3   **I am stressed because of my thin hair. _____(C)_____**

I know hair loss can hurt your confidence. But stress is one of the main reasons for hair loss. So rather than thinking about the problem, try to control your stress. Also, frequently using hair ties or getting chemical hair treatments can weaken your hair.

1 Match the correct question to blanks (A)~(C).

(1) (A) •   • ① Is this teenage hair loss?

(2) (B) •   • ② Should I tie it up or get a perm?

(3) (C) •   • ③ Are there any foods for preventing hair loss?

2 Where would the following sentence best fit?

However, has your hair been thinning or falling out more often nowadays?

① ⓐ   ② ⓑ   ③ ⓒ   ④ ⓓ

3 To make your hair healthier, what can you add to your meals?

_____

4 What is the best choice for blank (D)?

① strong

② wet

③ unhealthy

④ long

5 What is NOT true about teenage hair loss?

① It happens because of changing hormone levels.

② It is affected by eating foods with few vitamins or minerals.

③ It causes stress and hurts confidence.

④ It can be prevented by tying up one's hair.

6 Write T if the statement is true and F if it's false.

(1) If the hair loss comes from a hormone problem, there's no need to see a doctor.

(2) Using a chemical hair treatment can be a reason for hair loss.

Every day, you lose 50 to 100 hairs. That sounds like a lot, but new hair grows when old hair falls out. However, when it doesn't grow back, you may be experiencing hair loss. To know if you have this problem, check for these signs. First, see if your forehead looks big because your hairline is higher than before. Thin hair at your hairline can also show hair loss. Another sign is a growing bald ⁵ spot in your hair. Look for any areas that are missing hair. Furthermore, pull or brush your hair to see if it easily comes out. Checking your hair can help you catch these early signs of hair loss. Then, you can get help from a doctor before it gets worse! ¹⁰

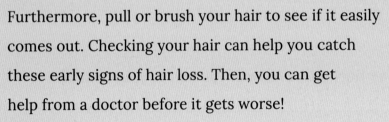

What is the passage mainly about?

① the cycle of growing hair

② the symptoms of hair loss

③ ways to manage damaged hair

④ how bad habits cause hair loss

⑤ the problems of having thin hair

Summary / Graphic Organizer

A Choose the correct words to fill in the blanks.

doctor	hormone	nutrition	hairline	chemical	confidence

Reading 1   Problems and Solutions for Teenage Hair Loss

My hair falls out because of changing _____ levels.

– Go to see a _____ and ask for help.

My hair looks unhealthy, as the _____ in my meals isn't enough.

– Have foods like fish and leafy vegetables.

I'm stressed about my thin hair, so I want to tie it up or get a perm.

– Stop thinking about the problem and control your stress.

– Using hair ties or _____ treatments is not helpful.

Reading 2

You can check for hair loss by looking at your _____, any areas of missing hair, or how easily your hair comes out.

Vocabulary

B Choose the correct word for each definition.

add	weaken	symptom	teenager	normal	forehead	bald

1 usual to what you expect it to be: _____

2 to make or become less strong or healthy: _____

3 having no hair on all or most of the head: _____

4 a physical or mental sign caused by sickness: _____

5 the part of your face between your eyes and hairline: _____

6 a young person who is from 13 to 19 years old: _____

Reading 1

Monkeys are like people in many ways. In fact, some of them even go to college! The Monkey College in Boston, Massachusetts, teaches the animals to become personal helpers for disabled people.

They chose *capuchin monkeys to be their "students" 5 for a few reasons. Firstly, they are very small but have a large brain. This makes them very smart. And they have very short tails. So, unlike other monkeys, they use their hands just like people do. _____(A)_____, these monkeys can live for up to forty years and get along well with humans. 10

The monkeys at the college begin their training when they are only a few months old. They start to learn simple tasks such as bringing food or picking things up. The training center is like a real house, with a microwave, a TV, and other household items. After several years of training, when the monkeys can perform more complicated tasks, they "graduate." ⓐ As every monkey has different talents, they 15 are carefully matched with their new owners. ⓑ Training monkeys is interesting but difficult. ⓒ So far, the results have been fantastic. ⓓ Most owners say their monkeys are not just helpers but also good friends.

*capuchin monkey: intelligent monkey that is native to Central and South America

1 **What is the best title for the passage?**

① How Monkeys Are like People

② Monkeys Give a Helping Hand

③ Special Animal Friends for Humans

④ When Monkeys and Humans Live Together

2 **What is the best choice for blank (A)?**

① However

② In addition

③ For example

④ Nevertheless

3 **What is NOT mentioned as a reason for choosing capuchin monkeys to be students at The Monkey College?**

① their large brains

② the way they use their hands

③ their long lifespan

④ their good health

4 **The monkeys start their training at the college when**

_____.

5 **Which sentence is NOT needed in the passage?**

① ⓐ   ② ⓑ   ③ ⓒ   ④ ⓓ

6 **What is NOT true about The Monkey College?**

① It helps disabled people by training monkeys.

② Monkeys are trained in their new owners' homes.

③ The training moves from easy tasks to more difficult ones.

④ It takes several years for a monkey to graduate.

Living with a Monkey Helper

By Carol E. Lee

Kristi (22-year-old)

Becky Thompson lost the use of her arms and legs in an accident. But her roommate Kristi helps her with everyday things Becky can't do. Kristi is a 22-year-old capuchin monkey! She was trained to bring Becky food and drinks, turn the pages of books, and even brush her teeth. Kristi ⁵ has greatly changed Becky's life. Becky compared it to the difference between living in black and white and living in color. "Kristi is more than just a helper. We know each other so well, and she always knows how I feel. Everything has been great since I met her," she said. ¹⁰

To summarize the passage, what is the best choice for blanks (A) and (B)?

A monkey named Kristi is not only a _____(A)_____ for Becky but also a _____(B)_____ friend.

	(A)		(B)
①	pet	—	good
②	helper	—	close
③	pet	—	trained
④	helper	—	disabled
⑤	doctor	—	loving

Summary / Graphic Organizer

A Choose the correct words to fill in the blanks.

people	hands	disabled	talent	helpers	simple

Reading 1

There is a special "college" in America that teaches capuchin monkeys to help _____ people. This type of monkey was chosen because they are very smart and use their _____ well. They also enjoy being with _____ and live for a long time. At first, the monkeys start learning _____ tasks. When they can do more complicated tasks, they "graduate" and go to live with a disabled person. Most of these people have been very happy with their new _____!

Vocabulary

B Choose the correct word for each definition.

disabled	tail	result	compare	several	complicated	graduate

1 more than two, but not many: _____

2 unable to use part of the body well: _____

3 something that happens because of something else: _____

4 to consider in relation to: _____

5 hard to explain or understand: _____

6 to earn a degree by completing school, university, or college: _____

Reading 1

You probably think zero is just a regular number. But it is not like all the other numbers. First of all, it was invented much later. ⓐ The numbers from 1 to 9 were invented thousands of years ago. ⓑ But the number zero was only created in the year 200 A.D. ⓒ People used stones to count 5 numbers at that time. ⓓ Why was that? It's because the idea of zero is difficult to understand.

To understand zero, you must realize that _____(A)_____. Is that confusing? Think about this example. When you take a class, you get a grade. If you 10 don't take the class, you get no grade—nothing. But what if you take the class and do very poorly? You could get a grade of zero.

Also, zero makes it easy to _____(B)_____. Before zero, people put a space when they wrote one thousand six, like "1 6." Thanks to zero, we write one thousand six as 15 "1,006" and can clearly see that it is different from 106 or 16. Truly, zero is a very important number!

1   **What is the best title for the passage?**

① Zero: A Very Special Number

② Different Uses of Zero in the Past

③ The World of Interesting Numbers

④ Regular Numbers vs. Special Numbers

2   **Which sentence is NOT needed in the passage?**

① ⓐ   ② ⓑ   ③ ⓒ   ④ ⓓ

3   **It took so long to invent the number zero because** _____

_____ .

4   **What is the best choice for blank (A)?**

① it is more than a number

② it's different from nothing

③ it's a number, not a letter

④ it's like getting grades in class

5   **What is the best choice for blank (B)?**

① count faster

② add two numbers

③ write large numbers

④ put spaces between numbers

6   **Write T if the statement is true and F if it's false.**

(1) If you do very poorly on a test, you could get no grade.

(2) We can easily understand large numbers because of zero.

Roman *numerals are numbers that look like letters from the alphabet. In this system, I is used for 1, V for five, X for 10, L for 50, C for 100, D for 500, and M for 1,000. They were used throughout Europe until Arabic numerals were created. (ⓐ) While Roman numerals still appear today on things like clocks and calendars, they aren't used for math now. (ⓑ) And the reader must add all the letters to know the total number. (ⓒ) Take MMDCCXIII, for example. (ⓓ) This means 1,000+1,000+500+100+100+10+1+1+1, or 2,713. (ⓔ) Thank goodness math tests don't use Roman numerals!

*numeral: the symbol used to represent a number

Where would the following sentence best fit?

That's because they are long and difficult.

① ⓐ   ② ⓑ   ③ ⓒ   ④ ⓓ   ⑤ ⓔ

Summary / Graphic Organizer

A Choose the correct words to fill in the blanks.

large	regular	difficult	special	spaces	nothing	later

Reading 1

Zero is a _____ number. It was added to our number system much _____ than the other numbers. That's because the idea of zero is not easy to understand. It's important to know that it is different from _____. If you don't take a class, you don't get a grade. You get nothing. But if you take the class and do very poorly, your grade will be zero. Zero also makes it easier to write _____ numbers. Before zero, people used _____ between the other numbers. But with zero, numbers like 1,006 are easy to understand!

Reading 2

Roman numerals are letters that represent numbers, but they are no longer used in math since they are too _____.

Vocabulary

B Choose the correct word for each definition.

invent	appear	grade	letter	system	total	confusing

1 to make, design, or think of a new thing: _____

2 not clear, difficult to understand: _____

3 a symbol used for writing words: _____

4 to be seen somewhere: _____

5 a letter or number given to show how good something is: _____

6 with everything included: _____

Reading 1

The cuckoo is a bird that makes a sound like its name: "Cuckoo! Cuckoo!" The soft cry might sound friendly and sweet, but cuckoos play a trick on other birds: They lay their eggs in other birds' nests.

A mother cuckoo lays 20 eggs, placing each one in a ⁵ different nest. (ⓐ) It chooses nests with eggs that are similar in size and color. (ⓑ) The mother cuckoo flies into the bird's nest, lays its own egg, and then quickly flies away. (ⓒ) The mother cuckoo lays many eggs this way. (ⓓ) ₁₀

Not only is the mother cuckoo an unwanted guest, but the baby cuckoo is also a _____(A)_____. Cuckoo chicks usually hatch first, and they don't like to share the nest or food! Cuckoo chicks are big, so it is easy for them to roll the other eggs and chicks out of the nest with their legs. The parents then forget about them and ₁₅ take care of the cuckoo chick. Because the cuckoo chick is a big eater, the parent birds work hard to give it food. Clearly, cuckoos sound better than they behave!

24

1 **What is the best title for the passage?**

① Love Each Other like Cuckoos

② The Cuckoo: An Uninvited Guest

③ When a Cuckoo Family Becomes Large

④ The Cuckoo: The Hardest-Working Bird

2 **When laying eggs, the mother cuckoo looks for nests with eggs that are _____.**

3 **Where would the following sentence best fit?**

Then it waits until the host bird leaves for food.

① ⓐ   ② ⓑ   ③ ⓒ   ④ ⓓ

4 **What is the best choice for blank (A)?**

① bad visitor

② secret helper

③ special friend

④ welcomed child

5 **What is suggested about the cuckoo's egg trick?**

① Cuckoos stay in the nests of other birds after laying their eggs.

② Cuckoos take the eggs of other birds and act like their parents.

③ Cuckoos make different kinds of sounds to keep their eggs safe.

④ Cuckoos lay eggs in other nests so that other birds raise cuckoo chicks.

6 **Write T if the statement is true and F if it's false.**

(1) A young cuckoo is big enough to push out other eggs or chicks.

(2) The parent birds roll the baby cuckoo out of the nest as soon as it starts hatching.

Cuckoos appear in many legends of Europe. In Britain, people think that the cuckoo's first call brings spring. Each year, major newspapers report the cuckoo's first calls. In Russia, people believe that the cuckoo knows how long a person will live. If someone hears a cuckoo's call in the woods, he or she asks, "Cuckoo, cuckoo, how long will I live?" It is believed that the person will live 5 one more year for each time the bird calls out "Cuckoo!" in return. In France, a legend says it is good luck to hear the first cuckoo call of spring when you have money in your pocket. If you do, you will be rich all year!

What is the passage mainly about?

① the role of cuckoos in the woods

② how cuckoos bring good or bad luck

③ some interesting legends about cuckoos

④ cuckoos' influence on European languages

⑤ the reason why people think cuckoos bring good luck

Summary / Graphic Organizer

A Choose the correct words to fill in the blanks.

| lays | feeding | big | meaning | choose | sound | trick |

Reading 1

The cuckoo is a bird that gets its name from the friendly _____ it makes. However, cuckoos play a mean _____ on other birds. A mother cuckoo _____ its eggs in other birds' nests. When the other birds are away, she flies over and lays one egg in each nest. When the cuckoo's egg hatches, the baby cuckoo is _____ enough to push out the other eggs and babies. Since cuckoo chicks eat a lot, the other birds are tricked into spending all their time _____ the cuckoo bird's baby.

Reading 2

In many European countries, the cuckoo's call has a special _____.

Vocabulary

B Choose the correct word for each definition.

| similar | chick | major | hatch | legend | roll | call out |

1 very large or important: _____

2 a baby bird: _____

3 an old story about famous people or events in the past: _____

4 to come out of an egg: _____

5 to move by turning over and over on a surface: _____

6 almost the same, but somewhat different: _____

UNIT 06 Literature

Reading 1

Saturday morning came. The summer was full of life. Everything was bright and fresh, but…

Tom came outside with a can of white paint and a brush. His aunt had angrily told him to paint the fence as a punishment for skipping school. With a sigh, he began to paint. 5

Soon a boy named Ben came along, eating an apple. Ben was a mean boy who always teased Tom. He stopped beside Tom and said, "Hey, Tom. You must be in trouble. You have to work!"

Tom looked at him for a moment and said, "What do you mean, 'work'?" 10

"Isn't that work?" asked Ben.

"Not at all! How often does a boy get a chance to _____(A)_____?"

Ben stopped eating the apple and watched Tom, who pretended to love every minute of painting the fence. Ben started to get more interested. He said, "Tom, let me try."

"No, no. Only I can do it. No other boy in the world can paint as well as me." 15

"Please let me try," begged Ben. "I'll give you my apple!"

At last, Tom agreed with a long face, but with a joyous heart. He sat down to eat the apple while Ben started to work.

28

1 **What is the best title for the passage?**

① Tom's Best Friend, Ben

② Tom Plays a Trick on Ben

③ Tom Meets a New Friend

④ Too Busy to Go to School

2 **Why did Tom's aunt punish Tom?**

_____

3 **What is the best choice for blank (A)?**

① skip school

② paint a fence

③ eat someone's apple

④ watch someone painting

4 **How did Tom make Ben paint the fence?**

① He pretended to be too sick to keep painting it.

② He told Ben that he would do anything if Ben painted it.

③ He acted like painting was a very interesting and fun job.

④ He promised to give an apple to Ben when it was finished.

5 **It can be inferred from the underlined sentence that**

_____.

① Tom was very clever

② Tom enjoyed painting

③ Tom had a joyous face

④ Tom was worried about Ben

6 **How did Tom's feelings change during the story?**

① sad → angry

② happy → lonely

③ disappointed → glad

④ proud → embarrassed

Mark Twain is one of America's best-loved writers. His novels, especially *The Adventures of Tom Sawyer* (1876) and *The Adventures of Huckleberry Finn* (1885), are still very popular. *The Adventures of Tom Sawyer* is based on Twain's childhood experiences. ⓐ It is about 5 the life of a playful boy living near the Mississippi River. ⓑ But Twain wasn't the only famous writer of his day to grow up in Mississippi. ⓒ Its story of friendship, first love, and adventure shows readers the joy of being a young boy. ⓓ *The Adventures of Huckleberry Finn* is about a boy called 10 Huck who runs away from his father with a black slave, Jim. ⓔ More serious than *The Adventures of Tom Sawyer*, it shows the friendship between Huck and Jim during many great adventures.

Which sentence is NOT needed in the passage?

① ⓐ   ② ⓑ   ③ ⓒ   ④ ⓓ   ⑤ ⓔ

Summary / Graphic Organizer

A Choose the correct words to fill in the blanks.

| adventures | tricked | tease | punished | fun | sigh |

Reading 1

It was a beautiful day, but Tom was being _____ for skipping school. His aunt said he had to paint a fence. While he was painting, a boy named Ben came by. He started to _____ Tom about being in trouble. But Tom pretended he wasn't being punished. He acted like painting the fence was very _____. Soon Ben wanted to paint the fence too. He gave Tom an apple to let him paint. Tom had _____ Ben into doing his work!

Reading 2

Mark Twain is a famous American writer who wrote stories about the _____ of young boys.

Vocabulary

B Choose the correct word for each definition.

| agree | tease | slave | adventure | serious | beg | skip |

1 to not do something that you usually do or should do: _____

2 to strongly ask someone to do something for you: _____

3 someone who is made to work for no money: _____

4 an exciting, unusual and sometimes dangerous experience: _____

5 so bad or dangerous that it's worrying: _____

6 to laugh at somebody and make jokes about them: _____

The Economy

Reading 1

Christmas is an important time for sharing and celebration. So when Christmas is coming, Americans are always busy with buying presents.

However, for some years, a weak economy made <u>this</u> hard. (ⓐ) So, The Carlisle Trust Company of Pennsylvania ⁵ started offering Christmas clubs in 1909. (ⓑ) A Christmas club was a savings account for holiday spending. (ⓒ) Bank customers put in some money into the account every week, and they only took it out for Christmas. (ⓓ) Over time, the bank even gave interest—or, money—for using their ¹⁰ service. So without worry, people could save money before they needed it.

While Christmas clubs were popular during bad economic times, they are not common these days. People say that Christmas clubs aren't useful. This is because banks offer low interest rates and have people pay to take out money. Only some community banks still offer them. ¹⁵

But even after a hundred years, one thing has remained the same: we still love giving Christmas gifts to our loved ones.
So, how about _____(A)_____ for Christmas early?

1   What is the passage mainly about?

① people saving money for Christmas

② the problems of spending during holidays

③ a special account made for the Christmas season

④ the reason for the economic difficulties in the 1900s

2   What does the underlined this refer to?

① spending money to buy presents

② saving money for Christmas presents

③ celebrating Christmas with family members

④ making a bank account before the holidays

3   Where would the following sentence best fit?

> During that time, people had trouble buying gifts, and some
> even had to borrow money from the bank!

① ⓐ   ② ⓑ   ③ ⓒ   ④ ⓓ

4   Some people say Christmas clubs are not useful, because banks

_____ .

5   What is NOT true about Christmas clubs?

① They are for people who want to save for the holidays.

② Customers can take out their money when Christmas is coming.

③ Banks offer interest to the customers who use its Christmas club.

④ Almost every bank in America is still offering them.

6   What is the best choice for blank (A)?

① saving money

② buying presents

③ taking out money

④ gathering together

Money can be difficult to manage. It's easy to spend, but it's not so easy to save. So it's important to manage your spending carefully. First, decide on how much money you want to save. (ⓐ) If you set a goal for yourself, it will be easier to limit your spending. (ⓑ) Then make a list of things you need to buy and another list of things you want to buy. (ⓒ) Finally, use a notebook or savings application to record what you spend. (ⓓ) This will help you remember your purchases and see how much you've saved. (ⓔ) By following these easy tips, you can manage your money confidently. ⁵

Where would the following sentence best fit?

This way, you can focus on necessary items first.

① ⓐ   ② ⓑ   ③ ⓒ   ④ ⓓ   ⑤ ⓔ

Summary / Graphic Organizer

A Choose the correct words to fill in the blanks.

customers	interest	economy	accounts	common	record

Reading 1

In the 1900s, the American _____ was bad, so people couldn't buy presents for Christmas. One trust company in Pennsylvania started to offer Christmas clubs to help them. _____ could put money into a savings account every week until it was Christmas. They would even get _____ from the bank! By Christmas, they would have enough money to buy presents. Nowadays, Christmas clubs aren't popular, though, because many people think they are useless. So they aren't _____ in banks anymore.

Reading 2

To manage your spending effectively, decide how much you want to save, focus on buying necessary items first, and _____ your purchases.

Vocabulary

B Choose the correct word for each definition.

save	decide	popular	record	gather	useful	tip

1 to keep something, like money, for the future: _____

2 to come or bring together: _____

3 able to be used in a helpful way: _____

4 a helpful piece of information: _____

5 to choose what you will do: _____

6 liked by many people: _____

UNIT 08 Science

Reading 1

Dear Dr. Kay,

　　Farting is so embarrassing. Yesterday I farted in class and everybody heard it! But I don't know _____(A)_____. Can you explain it? And is it better to hold farts in or to let them out?

Simon ⁵

　　I'm sorry to hear your embarrassing story. But don't be too embarrassed. After all, everybody farts. Even your principal farts. So does the Queen of England. Most people fart fourteen times a day. And here's why.

　After you eat a meal, your body breaks down the food. Inside your belly are ¹⁰ billions of tiny bacteria. They eat up the food. As they eat, they make gases. Some of these gases, such as ammonia, smell very bad. Certain foods make more gas than others. Foods such as vegetables and beans make a lot of gas.

　Farts can also be made by swallowing air. (ⓐ) This can happen when you eat too quickly or drink too much soda. (ⓑ) Some of the air comes out as a burp. (ⓒ) ¹⁵ But a lot of air goes to your belly and comes out as a fart. (ⓓ)

　Of course, it is not good manners to fart in front of others. But be careful of holding them in! If you do that, the gas may give you a bellyache. So, let your farts fly!

Dr. Kay

1 **What is the best choice for blank (A)?**

① what makes people fart

② why most farts smell bad

③ what people think of farts

④ how often most people fart

2 **Why does Dr. Kay mention <u>the Queen of England</u>?**

① to show that everybody farts

② to show how embarrassing farting is

③ to explain how many times women fart

④ to give an example of cultural differences

3 **Put the following in the correct order.**

You eat a meal. → ____(A)____ → ____(B)____ → ____(C)____

(1) (A) •   • ① You let out farts.

(2) (B) •   • ② Different gases are created.

(3) (C) •   • ③ The food is broken down.

4 **Where would the following sentence best fit?**

And some comes out of your lungs when you breathe.

① ⓐ   ② ⓑ   ③ ⓒ   ④ ⓓ

5 **You should be careful about holding farts in because _____**

_____ .

6 **According to Dr. Kay, which of the following can affect farts? (Choose two.)**

① how fast you eat

② how often you eat

③ what you do after eating

④ what kinds of food you eat

Why are some farts loud and others quiet? The loudness of a fart depends on the amount of gas.

(A) It is not true that loud farts are always smellier than quiet ones. In fact, a fart's smell depends on the type of food that is eaten.

5

(B) Eggs, milk, and meat create very smelly gas. Beans and vegetables, on the other hand, create large amounts of non-smelly gas.

(C) The more gas you let out, the louder your fart will be. Interestingly, however, a fart's sound is not related to its smell.

Choose the best order of (A), (B), and (C) after the given text.

① (A) – (C) – (B)
② (B) – (A) – (C)
③ (B) – (C) – (A)
④ (C) – (A) – (B)
⑤ (C) – (B) – (A)

Summary / Graphic Organizer

A   Choose the correct words to fill in the blanks.

| bacteria | reason | meal | bellyache | smell | normal | quickly |

Reading 1

Question	1. What is the _____ for farts? 2. Should farts be held in or let out?

▼

Answer	1. Farting is _____. • When _____ in your stomach eat food, they create gases. • When you eat too _____ or drink a lot of soda, you swallow air. 2. Holding them in can give you a _____.

Reading 2

While the loudness of a fart depends on the amount of gas, the _____ of a fart depends on what you eat.

Vocabulary

B   Choose the correct word for each definition.

| principal | tiny | swallow | amount | burp | manners | embarrassing |

1   the head of a school: _____

2   making you feel ashamed or anxious: _____

3   gas from the stomach that comes out through the mouth: _____

4   to make food, drink, etc. go down the throat into the stomach: _____

5   how much there is of something: _____

6   the proper way to act in a particular culture: _____

UNIT 09 Jobs

Reading 1

Welcome to the Antarctic! My name is Greg, and I am a weather scientist. For six months of the year, my team and I live here at the weather station. Our job is to observe the Antarctic weather and use that information to study how the climate will change in the future. 5

My day starts at seven a.m. It is still dark when I wake up. _____(A)_____, the sun never rises here in the winter. And in the summer, the sun never sets. After putting on my snowsuit, I walk to the research building. It is beside the ocean, so I often see fur seals and penguins. I take 10 measurements there every three hours until three p.m. My favorite job is launching the weather balloon. ⓐ I fill it with helium and send it into the sky. ⓑ The temperatures in the Antarctic go as low as -35°C. ⓒ The weather balloon has special equipment. ⓓ It measures air temperature and wind speed. In the evenings, we read books, talk, or watch movies. _____(B)_____, on some nights 15 we get a special treat: the auroras—beautiful colored lights in the night sky.

I think the South Pole is the most beautiful place on earth. And my job never gets boring on the icy 20 continent of Antarctica.

1 **What is the best title for the passage?**

① The Most Beautiful Place on Earth

② The Special Climate of the Antarctic

③ A Day in the Life of an Antarctic Scientist

④ What Is Good about Being a Weather Scientist?

2 **By observing the Antarctic weather, scientists can study**

_____.

3 **Which sentence is NOT needed in the passage?**

① ⓐ   ② ⓑ   ③ ⓒ   ④ ⓓ

4 **What is the best pair for blanks (A) and (B)?**

① Therefore   — In fact

② In fact   — However

③ For example — Therefore

④ However   — For example

5 **What is NOT mentioned about Greg in the passage?**

① what kinds of tasks he does

② how he spends his free time

③ how he feels about his job

④ how he became a weather scientist

6 **Write T if the statement is true and F if it's false.**

(1) Greg works alone at the weather station for half of the year.

(2) Greg often sees wild animals while he is working.

(3) Greg checks the temperature and wind speed until midnight.

The North and South Poles are quiet, beautiful places. They are so cold that few people or animals live there. Both poles are rich in natural oil, gas, and minerals. (ⓐ) So who owns them? (ⓑ) Actually, no country can own the poles. (ⓒ) Today, a total of thirty countries have research stations at the poles. (ⓓ) Thousands of scientists study the weather and wildlife in these freezing ⁵ regions. (ⓔ) They can carry out any research, but all of them have to follow one strict rule: They must not leave any waste or pollution or do anything else to damage the beautiful polar environment.

Where would the following sentence best fit?

Instead, countries can have research stations there.

① ⓐ   ② ⓑ   ③ ⓒ   ④ ⓓ   ⑤ ⓔ

Summary / Graphic Organizer

A Choose the correct words to fill in the blanks.

damage	change	balloon	snowsuit	carry out	measurements

Reading 1

Greg is a scientist who works in a weather station in the Antarctic. His main job is to observe weather and study climate _____. He wakes up at 7 a.m. and puts on his _____. Then he walks over to a research building. There, he takes _____ until 3 p.m. He sends a weather _____ into the sky to check air temperature and wind speed. At night, he reads books and talks with his team. Sometimes he gets a special treat — the beautiful light of the auroras.

Reading 2

No one country owns the North or South Poles, but many countries _____ research in these locations.

Vocabulary

B Choose the correct word for each definition.

pole	wildlife	observe	continent	treat	launch	temperature

1 to send something into the air or into space: _____

2 animals and plants that are found in nature: _____

3 to watch or study something or someone carefully: _____

4 something that gives you lots of pleasure and is usually unexpected: _____

5 one of the large areas of land on Earth like Europe or Asia: _____

6 the measurement of how hot or cold something is: _____

• Before Reading   What comes to your mind when you hear of "Hong Kong"?

Reading 1

Hong Kong is a unique place with a mixed culture. ⓐ It is a special region of China, so it follows many Chinese traditions. ⓑ But it is also influenced by Western culture. ⓒ This is because Hong Kong was controlled by England from 1841 to 1997. ⓓ Hong Kong is located on the southeast 5 coast of China. As a result, the culture of Hong Kong is diverse, and the people are open-minded.

When Hong Kong was under England's control, the only official language was English. However, many of the people in Hong Kong come from the Canton region in China. So 10 their language was also commonly used. And nowadays, both Chinese and English are used as official languages.

Hong Kong also celebrates both Chinese and Western holidays. For example, Chinese holidays such as Lunar New Year and the Mid-Autumn Festival are big celebrations for the people of Hong Kong. But they also celebrate Western holidays 15 such as Easter and Christmas.

Because of its _____(A)_____, Hong Kong follows both Eastern and Western traditions. It has a special culture, and the people come from many different backgrounds.

1 **What is the best title for the passage?**

① Visit Hong Kong for the Best Holiday!

② How Language Changed in Hong Kong

③ Hong Kong: A Unique Blend of Cultures

④ Unknown Facts about People in Hong Kong

2 **Which sentence is NOT needed in the passage?**

① ⓐ   ② ⓑ   ③ ⓒ   ④ ⓓ

3 **What can be inferred from the 2nd paragraph?**

① People from Canton did not want to speak in Chinese.

② Chinese was added as an official language of Hong Kong.

③ After the end of England's control over Hong Kong, English was not used anymore.

④ There were many English people in Hong Kong before it was under England's control.

4 **What is mentioned as examples of Hong Kong's diverse culture? (Choose two.)**

① art   ② festivals

③ holidays   ④ language

5 **What is the best choice for blank (A)?**

① laws   ② history

③ location   ④ influence

6 **Write T if the statement is true and F if it's false.**

(1) In Hong Kong, Chinese holidays are not very important.

(2) People in Hong Kong are from many different backgrounds.

Food from Hong Kong often shows its unique culture. Cha chaan tengs, Hong Kong-style cafés, are a great example of this. Because they were once under British control, people in Hong Kong started to add Western eating habits into their daily lives. However, for common workers, Western restaurants were too expensive. So cha chaan tengs were created. In the West, eating cake and drinking tea with milk was common. Cha chaan tengs used these ideas to make drinks and dishes like milk tea, pineapple buns, and egg tarts. As the food was so cheap, these cafés became more and more popular. Now, some dishes are even seen as important parts of Hong Kong's cultural heritage.

What is the best title for the passage?

① From Cheap Dishes to Fancy Food

② Hong Kong: The Best Place to Enjoy Cafés

③ Why Cha Chaan Tengs Are Loved in the West

④ The Story of Hong Kong's Special Café Foods

⑤ How Hong Kong's Food Changed British People

Summary / Graphic Organizer

A Choose the correct words to fill in the blanks.

Chinese	celebrated	common	controlled	English	dishes

Reading 1

The Mixed Culture in Hong Kong

Historical Background	Hong Kong was _____ by England from 1841 to 1997.
Languages	- At first, the only official language was _____. - Later, _____ also became an official language due to a number of people from Canton.
Holidays	Both Chinese and Western holidays are _____.

Reading 2

The _____ sold at cha chaan tengs were inspired by Western eating habits, and they are important to Hong Kong's culture.

Vocabulary

B Choose the correct word for each definition.

cheap	fancy	unique	influence	location	coast	mixed

1 extremely decorated or complicated: _____

2 a place, area, or position: _____

3 the land close to the ocean: _____

4 made up of different things: _____

5 being so special that nothing else is like it: _____

6 to cause a change in how someone or something acts, thinks, or develops:

_____

UNIT 11 Issues

• **Before Reading**   Does your school use education apps in class?

Many students these days use education apps and websites to study at school. Some people welcome these new technologies. But others worry that the student data stored in them is not safe.

Jason

I think education apps and websites should ⁵ be used in schools. (ⓐ) They can let teachers know what students need more help in. (ⓑ) They can also help teachers make better lesson plans. (ⓒ) In the end, this will help students receive a better education. (ⓓ)   ¹⁰

Thomas

I don't think these new technologies should be used in schools. Since the data collected isn't stored by the school, it's not safe. The companies that create these programs don't care about students' privacy. In fact, student data has already been stolen by hackers.

Lisa

In my opinion, _____(A)_____ . If they only use ¹⁵ traditional teaching methods, students will become bored. And if students aren't interested, then they won't learn.

Angela

These new technologies do have many benefits. However, the most important thing is students' privacy. I think some policies should be made to protect student data.   ²⁰

1 **What is the best title for the passage?**

① How to Protect Your Privacy Online

② What Are the Best Education Apps?

③ Should Education Apps Be Used in Class?

④ How Mobile Apps Are Changing Education

2 **Where would the following sentence best fit?**

> The main reason is that they are helpful for teachers.

① ⓐ   ② ⓑ   ③ ⓒ   ④ ⓓ

3 **Why does Thomas think new technologies should not be used in class?**

① Education apps are expensive.

② Students' data can be used in the wrong way.

③ New technologies are not effective for learning.

④ Teachers are not used to using new technologies.

4 **What is the best choice for blank (A)?**

① students shouldn't use their cell phones during class

② teachers should respect traditional teaching methods

③ protecting students' privacy is the most important thing

④ schools should use as much new technology as possible

5 **Angela thinks some policies are needed to keep student data safe because** _____ .

6 **Who has the same opinion as the following sentence?**

> Thanks to some interesting education apps, students can enjoy studying.

① Thomas   ② Lisa   ③ Angela   ④ no one

Delete X

Web search engines are really good at finding and storing data. This makes the internet very helpful, but very bad if _____. That's why the "right to be forgotten" law has recently become an issue. This law will make internet companies remove data if someone requests it. It will help protect your privacy, but some ⁵ people say it will threaten the open nature of the internet and the free flow of information. While some countries have already accepted the "right to be forgotten" as a law, others are still debating the topic. But as some internet companies don't have to delete your data even if you ask, support for the "right to be forgotten" is growing. ¹⁰

What is the best choice for the blank?

① technological issues happen too often

② you cannot use the data when you need it

③ it's hard to trust the information you find online

④ you want to remove information about yourself

⑤ your private data is useless to internet companies

Summary / Graphic Organizer

A Choose the correct words to fill in the blanks.

privacy	remove	education	policy	interesting	stolen

Reading 1   Using Education Apps in Class

For

Jason: Teachers can prepare better lessons and students can get a better _____.

Lisa: Students will find learning _____.

Against

Thomas: Student data could be _____ by hackers.

Angela: New technologies could be dangerous if students' _____ is not protected.

Reading 2

The "right to be forgotten" is forcing some internet companies to _____ users' online data, but some worry it will make the internet less open.

Vocabulary

B Choose the correct word for each definition.

benefit	receive	store	delete	privacy	support	traditional

1 agreement with an idea: _____

2 the right to keep one's personal things secret: _____

3 something useful that you get from a thing or a situation: _____

4 to get something from someone: _____

5 to erase or remove information, especially written or typed words: _____

6 to keep something somewhere for future use: _____

• Before Reading   What spices do you like the most?

Reading 1

Cinnamon, garlic, ginger, and saffron... You can probably name a few spices. Spices are parts of plants, like leaves, flowers, or fruit. They have unique smells and tastes, so people use them to add flavor to their food.

But spices also do something more important. Spices 5 keep food from going bad. This is because spices have powerful chemicals. These chemicals protect the spice plants from bacteria, insects, and hungry animals. When we use spices in food, the same chemicals do the same thing: They kill or slow the growth of dangerous bacteria that 10 make food go bad. Garlic, onion, and oregano are especially good at killing bacteria.

Therefore, it's not surprising that foods are spicier in places with hot weather, where foods go bad quickly. Countries like Ethiopia and India use more spices than any other country in the world. They usually have about six spices in each recipe. However, in Northern Europe, which usually has cold weather, many recipes have no 15 spices at all.

People in hot countries have a good reason for their love of spices. Spices make their food tastier and _____(A)_____!

1 **What is the best title for the passage?**

① The King of Spices

② A Secret Benefit of Spices

③ The Early History of Spices

④ Perfect Recipes for Spice Lovers

2 **People add spices to flavor their food because they have**

_____ .

3 **How do spices keep food from going bad?**

① Their sharp smell keeps bacteria away.

② They change the chemicals in the food.

③ Strong chemicals in them fight bacteria.

④ Chemicals in them keep food dry and cold.

4 **What is the 3rd paragraph mainly about?**

① which country first used spices

② why Europeans don't like spices

③ where most spices are produced

④ how weather and spice use are related

5 **What is the best choice for blank (A)?**

① safer ② softer

③ simpler ④ unhealthier

6 **According to the passage, what is NOT true?**

① Spices can be leaves, flowers, or the fruit of a plant.

② The powerful chemicals in spices are enjoyed by insects.

③ Garlic, onion, and oregano are very good at keeping food from going bad.

④ People in hot places eat more spices than people in cold places.

Pepper is a very common spice today. In the past, however, it was very valuable and even used as money.

(A) Later, pepper became cheap enough for everyone to buy. But it's still important, making up one fifth of the world's spice trade. ⁵

(B) And this spice search actually changed world history. It was pepper that led Christopher Columbus to discovering America. He started his travels in search of a new way to India, not new lands.

(C) Back then, one gram of pepper was sold for one gram of gold. So, in the 15th century, Europeans tried to find the shortest way to India, where pepper ¹⁰ was produced.

Choose the best order of (A), (B), and (C) after the given text.

① (A) – (C) – (B)

② (B) – (A) – (C)

③ (B) – (C) – (A)

④ (C) – (A) – (B)

⑤ (C) – (B) – (A)

Summary / Graphic Organizer

A Choose the correct words to fill in the blanks.

| plants   value   hotter   recipe   bacteria   unique |

Reading 1

Spices are made from parts of _____, such as their leaves, flowers, and fruit. They are used to add _____ smells and tastes to food. But they do something else as well. Chemicals in spices kill _____ that make food go bad. Therefore, spices can help food last longer. This is why countries in _____ parts of the world generally add more spices to their food.

Reading 2

The high _____ of pepper in the 15th century is the reason Columbus discovered America, but nowadays pepper is a common and cheap spice.

Vocabulary

B Choose the correct word for each definition.

| growth   add   flavor   discover   trade   insect   sharp |

1 an increase in size, development, or number: _____

2 any small animal that has six legs and a body with three parts: _____

3 buying and selling products between countries: _____

4 to find something or some place for the first time: _____

5 the particular way something tastes: _____

6 having a strong taste or smell: _____

The Environment

Reading 1

Imagine waking up in a hotel in Kenya. You have a full day of adventure planned. A guide will take you to see local animals, including elephants, lions, and zebras, in their natural habitats!

This is an example of ecotourism—a way of seeing the 5 wonders of the natural world up close without harming the environment. Every year, millions of people participate in ecotourism. Many people say that these activities help protect these areas. However, some researchers are _____(A)_____. They believe that tourists are causing 10 problems for animals. For example, sea turtles in Costa Rica recently had problems laying their eggs because too many tourists came to watch them.

Also, regular interaction with kind humans might cause animals to become less careful. This could make them easier targets for predators. Because of these negative effects, we need to take a careful approach to ecotourism. We must understand how 15 different species will respond to human visitors. And we must make sure that human contact does not put animals at risk in any way.

1 What is the passage mainly about?

① an example of ecotourism

② reasons why people travel

③ negative effects of ecotourism

④ how to interact with wild animals

2 According to the passage, ecotourism is _____.

① a campaign to protect endangered animals

② volunteer work involving planting trees for the environment

③ a way to visit beautiful parts of the world without causing damage

④ an activity in which tourists experience the lifestyle of local people

3 What is the best choice for blank (A)?

① encouraged   ② honest

③ faithful   ④ doubtful

4 Sea turtles in Costa Rica had trouble with laying their eggs

because _____.

5 What is mentioned as a negative effect of ecotourism?

① It is the main cause of global warming.

② It costs too much for tourists to participate in.

③ It is hard for tourists to concentrate on their trip.

④ It makes animals more likely to be killed by predators.

6 What does the writer suggest we do? (Choose two.)

① We should learn how animals react to humans.

② We should take a class to learn about wild animals.

③ We should wear special clothing to avoid harming nature.

④ We should make sure human contact is not a danger to animals.

Some people might point out the negative effects of ecotourism, but it also has many benefits. Some of its most positive effects are on the environment. Ecotourism helps people respect nature. This makes them ⁵ care more about protecting wildlife and natural areas. (ⓐ) For visitors, ecotourism offers great opportunities. (ⓑ) They can experience the beauty of the natural world. (ⓒ) They can also meet new people and learn about their cultures. (ⓓ) Ecotourism also creates jobs for local people. (ⓔ) This type of work can also help them be proud of their ¹⁰ community.

Where would the following sentence best fit?

| They can work as guides and share their knowledge with visitors. |

① ⓐ   ② ⓑ   ③ ⓒ   ④ ⓓ   ⑤ ⓔ

Summary / Graphic Organizer

A Choose the correct words to fill in the blanks.

| problems habitats respect interact careful imagine |

Reading 1

Ecotourism allows people to see the wonders of nature while conserving the environment. Many people say that this helps protect animals' natural _____, but others say tourists cause _____. For example, sea turtles in Costa Rica recently couldn't lay their eggs, because too many tourists came to watch them. Also, animals that regularly _____ with kind humans may be easier for predators to catch. Therefore, we must be _____ and only use ecotourism in a way that does not put animals in danger.

Reading 2

Ecotourism teaches people to _____ the environment, creates jobs, and helps locals feel proud of their culture.

Vocabulary

B Choose the correct word for each definition.

| predator doubtful area negative interaction harm positive |

1 having unpleasant or bad qualities: _____

2 a certain part of a town, city, or country: _____

3 an animal that kills and eats other animals: _____

4 to cause someone physical injury, usually on purpose: _____

5 having pleasant or good qualities: _____

6 uncertain or unlikely to happen or be true: _____

UNIT 14 People

Reading 1

Malala Yousafzai is known as an international symbol of peace and children's rights. When Malala was eleven years old, the Taliban took over her town in Pakistan. ⓐGirls were forbidden from getting an education. ⓑUnable to attend school, Malala kept a blog instead. ⓒA blog allows ⁵ visitors to leave comments and send messages. ⓓShe wrote that everyone has the right to an education. The Taliban wanted to stop her, so they sent someone to kill her. The man got on a truck that was taking Malala to school and shot her in the head. _____(A)_____, she survived. And she ¹⁰ refused to let the attack silence her.

Just nine months later, she gave a speech at the United Nations. She said, "They thought that the bullets would silence me. But they failed. Out of that silence came thousands of voices. Weakness, fear and hopelessness died. Strength, power, and courage were born." Her words inspired people ¹⁵ around the world. In 2011, she won her country's National Youth Peace Prize. And in 2014, she became the youngest person ever to win the Nobel Peace Prize.

Winning the Nobel Peace Prize encouraged ²⁰ Malala to continue her efforts. "This award is for all those children whose voices need to be heard," she said.

1 **What is the passage mainly about?**

① a girl who lost her family

② the violence of the Taliban

③ the history of the Nobel Prize

④ a girl who spoke out for children's rights

2 **What did Malala do when she couldn't go to school?**

① helped her mother do chores

② taught other students English

③ kept a diary about her daily life

④ wrote her thoughts on education in a blog

3 **Which sentence is NOT needed in the passage?**

① ⓐ   ② ⓑ   ③ ⓒ   ④ ⓓ

4 **What is the best choice for blank (A)?**

① In short

② Otherwise

③ Moreover

④ Fortunately

5 **According to Malala, what three things were created by the Taliban's attack?**

_____

6 **According to the passage, what is NOT true about Malala Yousafzai?**

① When eleven, she couldn't go to school.

② She was hit by a truck.

③ The Taliban almost killed her.

④ She is the youngest Nobel Peace Prize winner ever.

The first ever Youth Takeover of the UN took place on July 12, 2013. There were hundreds of representatives from all over the world at the event, but it was Malala's speech that got the world's attention.

Hello, everyone. My name is Malala, and I am honored to be speaking to you today. When we see darkness, we realize the importance of light; when we are ⁵ silenced, we come to know the value of our voice. It wasn't until I was faced with guns in Pakistan that I realized the importance of _____. Every woman and child struggling for their rights must pick up their most powerful weapons —books and pens. Together, one child, one teacher, one pen, and one book can change the world. ¹⁰

What is the best choice for the blank?

① health
② military
③ resources
④ education
⑤ community

Summary / Graphic Organizer

A Choose the correct words to fill in the blanks.

shot	survived	symbol	forbade	education	encouraged

Reading 1

When Malala Yousafzai was eleven years old, the Taliban took over her town. They _____ girls from going to school. So Malala kept a blog instead. She wrote that everyone has the right to a(n) _____. Then one day, she was _____ by a member of the Taliban. Fortunately, she _____, and she later gave an inspiring speech at the United Nations. In 2014, she became the youngest person ever to win the Nobel Peace Prize. Now she has become an international _____ of peace and children's rights.

Vocabulary

B Choose the correct word for each definition.

struggle	speech	weapon	value	refuse	weakness	international

1 an object that can hurt someone, such as a gun: _____

2 a formal talk about a specific subject to a group of people: _____

3 to firmly say no to something: _____

4 to make an effort to do something difficult: _____

5 between two or more countries: _____

6 a lack of strength or power in one's character: _____

Technology

Reading 1

Many people think that hackers are cybercriminals. These people think hackers just break into websites and computer systems, and cause problems for selfish reasons. These hackers are called black hat hackers. However, there is more than one type of hacker. 5

Other hackers are called white hat hackers. These hackers help people. The idea for these terms comes from old Western movies in America. In these movies, the heroes always wear white hats, and the bad guys wear black hats. In the same way, white hat hackers 10 _____(A)_____ harm while black hat hackers cause harm.

Black hat hackers steal important information from people, like bank account numbers and log-in details. And they use it to make money or to cause problems in society. White hat hackers use the same methods as black hat hackers, but they have permission to do it. Instead of stealing information from a system, they look for 15 weaknesses in its security. Then they help the owners fix those weaknesses. For this reason, these hackers are in high demand.

These days, cybercrimes are becoming very common. That's why white hat hackers are important. They help protect important information and keep 20 people safe online.

1 **What is the passage mainly about?**

① what a white hat hacker is

② the danger of cybercrimes

③ how to be a black hat hacker

④ how hackers became popular

2 **Where did the terms "white hat hackers" and "black hat hackers" come from?**

_____

3 **What is the best choice for blank (A)?**

① make   ② do

③ prevent   ④ accept

4 **What is NOT true about hackers?**

① Hackers enter internet and computer systems.

② Black hat hackers cause trouble without a care for others.

③ White hat hackers find weaknesses in a system.

④ White hat hackers are not wanted by many people.

5 **What is the best pair for blanks (B) and (C)?**

Though hackers use _____(B)_____ methods, they have _____(C)_____ reasons for hacking.

	(B)		(C)
①	similar	—	good
②	common	—	selfish
③	the same	—	different
④	direct	—	opposite

6 **What is NOT mentioned in the passage?**

① Not all hackers are cybercriminals.

② Bad guys used black hats in classic Western movies.

③ White hat hackers work with the owners of computer systems.

④ Black hat hackers are important for online security.

Hackers are a constant threat to people using the internet. Thankfully, there are easy ways to lower your chances of being hacked. First of all, learn how to recognize phishing emails. If you don't recognize a sender's email address, just delete the email. And never click on links or download programs from it. Second, delete your search history regularly. ⓐThis ⁵ prevents hackers from gathering information about your online life. ⓑYour online life enables you to access a wide variety of information. ⓒFinally, turn your computer or device off when you don't need it. ⓓIt's harder for hackers to target you if you aren't online. ⓔWith these simple tips, you can avoid online threats and keep your information safe. ¹⁰

Which sentence is NOT needed in the passage?

① ⓐ   ② ⓑ   ③ ⓒ   ④ ⓓ   ⑤ ⓔ

Summary / Graphic Organizer

A Choose the correct words to fill in the blanks.

safe	selfish	enter	weaknesses	gathering	deleting

Reading 1

Hackers	_____ websites and computer systems

Black Hat Hackers	- cause problems for _____ reasons - steal important information from people

White Hat Hackers	- prevent harm and keep people _____ online - look for _____ in systems and help fix them

Reading 2

You can limit your chances of being hacked by learning how to identify phishing emails, _____ your search history regularly, and turning off your device when you don't need it.

Vocabulary

B Choose the correct word for each definition.

permission	account	constant	selfish	threat	hero	lower

1 a person, thing, or situation that could hurt you: _____

2 the ability to do something because someone allowed you to do it: _____

3 always or repeatedly happening: _____

4 someone who is respected for their brave or good actions: _____

5 to make something less in number, value, or amount: _____

6 caring only about your own needs and wishes: _____

UNIT 16 Entertainment

• Before Reading　Do you think vegetables can be used as instruments?

Reading 1

Carrots, peppers, pumpkins—most people use these vegetables to make their dinner. However, for the Vienna Vegetable Orchestra, they are perfect instruments for playing music! Since 1998, this group of thirteen men and women has been making music with vegetables and giving ⁵ concerts around the world.

It is a concert day. ⓐ The musicians are at the local market. ⓑ They are looking for good, fresh "instruments" to buy. ⓒ After shopping, they begin making instruments. ⓓ Fresh vegetables are an important part of a healthy diet. ¹⁰ With just a knife, a drill, and imagination, soon there will be a carrot flute, a pepper trumpet, and a pumpkin drum! Now, it's time to play. The concert starts and the audience is surprised: How can the vegetables produce such a calm and comforting sound? It's a unique sound that no other instruments can make. In addition, fresh smells from the vegetables fill the whole concert hall. ¹⁵

The performance is over, but no one leaves the concert hall. Why? They're waiting for some vegetable soup that is made from the instruments! This special orchestra pleases not only your ears, but your nose and stomach too.

1 **What is the best title for the passage?**

① Good Vegetables for Musicians

② A Dinner Party with an Orchestra

③ The World's Most Popular Orchestra

④ An Interesting Orchestra with Tasty Instruments

2 **Which sentence is NOT needed in the passage?**

① ⓐ   ② ⓑ   ③ ⓒ   ④ ⓓ

3 **The underlined sentence suggests that making vegetable instruments is _____.**

① easy and boring

② quick and simple

③ hard but interesting

④ dangerous but important

4 **What is NOT true about the vegetable orchestra?**

① The musicians try to buy expensive vegetables to make instruments.

② Its members make their own instruments.

③ It surprises the audience with its calm and comforting sound.

④ The audience can smell the vegetables during the performance.

5 **According to the passage, people stay in the hall after the concert is over because _____**

_____ .

6 **It can be inferred from the passage that _____.**

① the concerts are held at dinner time

② the vegetable soup doesn't taste very good

③ there are other vegetable orchestras in the world

④ the musicians use new instruments for every concert

An interview with a member of the Vienna Vegetable Orchestra

Q _____

A Vegetables sound great, and you can also smell and taste them. They're nice to look at too, with many different colors and shapes. Most importantly, you can find them anywhere.

Q Are all of you vegetarians? 5

A Oh, we hear that question too often! No, we're not.

Q Is it difficult to prepare for your concerts?

A Sometimes it's hard to find the right vegetables. To make a carrot recorder, for example, you need a special kind of carrot. In some countries, it can be hard to find.

Q How do all the members work with each other? 10

A There are thirteen of us and we all have different ideas about music. Therefore, we talk a lot during practice. In this way, we respect each other's ideas.

What is the best choice for the blank?

① Where do you get your instrument from?

② How do you turn vegetables into musical instruments?

③ Who first thought of organizing the vegetable orchestra?

④ What are the reasons you use vegetables as instruments?

⑤ What is needed to make vegetables that can be used as instruments?

Summary / Graphic Organizer

A Choose the correct words to fill in the blanks.

instruments	shopping	soup	concerts	markets

Reading 1

The Vienna Vegetable Orchestra travels around the world giving _____.
It's very special because all its _____ are made from vegetables. The
members buy the vegetables from local _____ on the day of each
concert. Then they turn them into instruments. The music is calm and relaxing,
and the vegetables smell great. After the concert, the instruments are made into
vegetable _____, which is shared with the audience.

Vocabulary

B Choose the correct word for each definition.

calm	imagination	fill	audience	please	diet	shape

1 to make something full: _____

2 to make someone feel happy: _____

3 food or drink that you regularly eat or drink: _____

4 a group of people who have come to a place to watch or listen to something:

_____

5 the outline or form of someone or something: _____

6 not showing or feeling strong emotions: _____

UNIT *17* The Arts

Reading 1

When we think of ancient Egypt, we imagine the great pyramids. But ancient Egyptians also made many kinds of art, including paintings. Egyptian painters followed the same rules for more than 3,500 years! So it's easy to recognize the ancient Egyptian style. 5

Egyptian painters often painted people. However, the people they painted didn't look very _____(A)_____. If you try to stand like them, you would fall over! The painters drew each part of the body from its best-looking angle. The head was drawn from the side so the shape of the nose 10 and mouth could be seen. But the eye was drawn from the front because it looked most interesting that way. The upper body was also drawn from the front. The legs, however, were drawn from the side like the person was walking.

There were rules about the size of a person too. Size was used to show how important the person was. Of course, kings appeared very large in paintings. But 15 when the gods were painted, their size was even greater.

Now, with these rules in mind, Egyptian paintings should be more interesting to look at.

72

1   **What is the passage mainly about?**

① the life of Egyptian painters

② the rules of Egyptian paintings

③ the importance of Egyptian art

④ the history of Egyptian paintings

2   **We easily recognize the ancient Egyptian style because**

_____ .

3   **What is the best choice for blank (A)?**

① interesting   ② ancient

③ realistic   ④ handsome

4   **In the 2nd paragraph, the writer explains how people were painted by** _____ .

① describing each part of the body

② showing various styles of paintings

③ introducing famous Egyptian painters

④ giving examples of different paintings

5   **What can be inferred from the 3rd paragraph?**

① Egyptians were interested in beauty.

② Egyptian kings liked to paint themselves.

③ Large paintings were very popular in ancient Egypt.

④ Egyptians thought gods were more important than kings.

6   **Write T if the statement is true and F if it's false.**

(1) The heads of Egyptians were drawn from the front — it's the best-looking angle.

(2) Egyptian painters painted people's legs from the side.

Colors were very important in Egyptian paintings. Artists used only six colors. These colors had special meanings. Red was the color of power and fire. Green showed nature and new life. Blue was the color of the sky and imagination. Yellow was for the sun and long life. White showed pure beauty, and black showed death. Artists always painted gods and goddesses certain ⁵ colors. For example, Osiris, the god of plants and birth, was always painted green. Nut, the sky goddess, was always painted blue.

To summarize the passage, what is the best choice for blanks (A) and (B)?

Six colors were used in Egyptian paintings to show different _____(A)_____, especially for their _____(B)_____.

	(A)		(B)
①	stories	—	jobs
②	topics	—	artists
③	people	—	families
④	feelings	—	kings
⑤	meanings	—	gods

Summary / Graphic Organizer

A Choose the correct words to fill in the blanks.

front	rules	gods	recognize	size	angles

Reading 1

It's easy to _____ the ancient Egyptian style.

▲

1. Body parts were painted at different _____ to make them look good.
   - Eyes and upper bodies were painted from the _____.
   - Heads and legs were painted from the side.

✚

2. _____ was used to show a person's importance.
   - Kings were painted larger than normal people.
   - _____ were painted even larger than kings.

Vocabulary

B Choose the correct word for each definition.

follow	side	angle	pure	upper	ancient	draw

1 higher than something else: _____

2 to do something in the way you are told: _____

3 the part of something that is not the front or back: _____

4 the direction from which you look at something: _____

5 not mixed with anything different from itself: _____

6 from many years ago: _____

Reading 1

A bell rings and two strong fighters step into a boxing ring. Can you guess what happens next? They sit down at a table and start to play chess! This is what happens in a popular new sport called chess boxing.

At the beginning of a chess boxing match, the fighters ⁵ play chess for four minutes. ⓐThen, they go to their corners and put on their boxing gloves. ⓑAfter the chessboard is taken away, a three-minute boxing round begins. ⓒThe ancient Greeks thought boxing was enjoyed by the gods, so it became part of the Olympic Games in ¹⁰ about 688 BC. ⓓThe fighters continue switching between chess and boxing for up to eleven rounds. The match ends if one of the fighters is knocked out. It also ends if a fighter loses the chess game or runs out of time while playing chess.

The first chess boxing competition was held in 2003 in Germany. Since then, the sport has spread to countries all over the world. Fighters prepare for a chess ¹⁵ boxing competition in different ways. One often-used method is switching between strength exercises and speed chess games. This helps the fighters get used to the unusual rhythm of a real match!

1 **What is the passage mainly about?**

① how to play chess boxing

② the origin of chess boxing

③ the health benefits of chess boxing

④ how to be a chess boxing champion

2 **Which sentence is NOT needed in the passage?**

① ⓐ   ② ⓑ   ③ ⓒ   ④ ⓓ

3 **What is NOT mentioned as a way for a chess boxing match to end?**

① when one of the fighters can't box anymore

② when one of the fighters loses the chess game

③ when one of the fighters loses more than six rounds

④ when one of the fighters runs out of time in the chess game

4 **What is NOT true about chess boxing?**

① Chess boxing is played in a boxing ring.

② Fighters box for four minutes.

③ There are eleven rounds in total.

④ Chess boxing competitions started in 2003.

5 **What is the best pair for blanks (A) and (B)?**

Germany held the ____(A)____ chess boxing competition, and the sport has since become ____(B)____ around the world.

① biggest – rare   ② first – popular

③ last – unpopular   ④ latest – common

6 **To prepare for a real match, fighters often train by _____**

_____ .

The idea for chess boxing originally came from the French cartoonist Enki Bilal's 1992 *graphic novel *Froid Équateur*. But the Dutch artist Iepe Rubingh turned this idea into a reality. In Bilal's graphic novel, a whole boxing match was held and then followed by a chess match. Rubingh changed the rules so that fighters switch between rounds of chess and boxing.

Over time, more and more people have become interested in chess boxing. Now, competitions are held in Europe, the United States, and Japan. Maybe there will soon be a chess boxing match near you!

*graphic novel: a novel in the form of a comic book

What is the passage mainly about?

① interesting rules for chess boxing

② European's great love for art and novels

③ the first chess boxing match in the world

④ the origin of chess boxing as a real game

⑤ the world's most famous chess boxing player

Summary / Graphic Organizer

A Choose the correct words to fill in the blanks.

follow	knocked	reality	prepare	switch	strength

Reading 1

In the popular new sport called chess boxing, fighters _____ between playing chess and boxing for up to eleven rounds. If one of the fighters is _____ out or loses the chess game, then the match ends. The first chess boxing competition was held in 2003 in Germany. Now, there are competitions all over the world. Fighters often _____ for a chess boxing competition by going back and forth between _____ exercises and speed chess games. This allows them to get used to the unusual rhythm of chess boxing.

Reading 2

Chess boxing was invented by French cartoonist Enki Bilal, and it became popular after Dutch artist Iepe Rubingh made it a _____.

Vocabulary

B Choose the correct word for each definition.

take away	match	continue	strength	spread	switch	originally

1 when something first occurred: _____

2 to remove something: _____

3 to move out across a large or increasing area: _____

4 a sports event in which people or teams compete: _____

5 to remain or go on without stopping: _____

6 to change from one person or thing to another: _____

Origins

Do you know when people started to wear T-shirts?

Reading 1

It's hard to imagine life without T-shirts. But T-shirts didn't become popular until the 1960s.

During World War I, American soldiers wore wool uniforms in the hot summer of Europe. They saw European soldiers wearing ⓐ cotton undershirts and started copying ⁵ their style. Because of their simple shape, they were called T-shirts. By World War II, both the US Army and the Navy included them in ⓑ their uniforms.

Up until the 1950s, T-shirts were still considered underwear. It was actors Marlon Brando and James Dean ¹⁰ who shocked audiences by wearing them in movies. People were surprised to see underwear worn as outerwear on the screen. James Dean made the T-shirt a symbol of cool youth when he wore ⓒ one in his movie A *Rebel Without a Cause*. And the tight style that showed his body soon became popular.

Developments in printing in the 1960s brought another change to T-shirts: ¹⁵ People started printing on them. ⓓ These inexpensive cotton canvases became a way for wearers to share their likes and dislikes. Since then, T-shirts have become even more popular. Why not? They are inexpensive, comfortable, stylish, and fun!

1   **What is the best title for the passage?**

① A Time without T-shirts

② A Short History of T-shirts

③ T-shirts: A Memory of the War

④ What's Your Favorite Type of T-shirt?

2   **World War I helped T-shirts _____.**

① become simple in shape

② be worn by young people

③ become popular in Europe

④ spread to American soldiers

3   **What made people see T-shirts as outerwear?**

① Soldiers brought T-shirts from Europe.

② Movie stars looked good in their T-shirts.

③ Famous designers began to make T-shirts.

④ A movie about T-shirts became successful.

4   **Which is NOT referring to the same thing?**

① ⓐ   ② ⓑ   ③ ⓒ   ④ ⓓ

5   **Thanks to developments in printing in the 1960s, people started to use T-shirts as a way to _____**

_____.

6   **Write T if the statement is true and F if it's false.**

(1) The name of T-shirts came from their simple shape.

(2) Because of James Dean, T-shirts were only worn by actors.

A tennis shirt, also known as a polo shirt, is a thick cotton T-shirt with a collar. It was invented by a French tennis champion, René Lacoste, in 1926.

(A) Soon his new design became popular with other tennis players. In the 1930s, even polo players began to wear it as part of their uniform.

(B) Today, this tennis shirt, or polo shirt, is not just for sports players. It has become everyday fashion for everyone.

5

(C) At that time, tennis players usually wore long-sleeved shirts and ties. Lacoste thought they were too hot and uncomfortable. So he designed a new tennis shirt and wore it in a game.

Choose the best order of (A), (B), and (C) after the given text.

① (A) – (C) – (B)

② (B) – (A) – (C)

③ (B) – (C) – (A)

④ (C) – (A) – (B)

⑤ (C) – (B) – (A)

Summary / Graphic Organizer

A Choose the correct words to fill in the blanks.

showing	outerwear	uncomfortable	print	soldiers	shape

Reading 1

During World War I, Americans saw Europeans wearing cotton undershirts.

→ T-shirts became popular with American _____.

▼

In the 1950s, actors began to wear them as _____ in movies.

→ T-shirts became popular with young people.

▼

In the 1960s, it became possible to _____ on T-shirts.

→ T-shirts became a way of _____ someone's ideas.

Reading 2

René Lacoste invented the polo shirt, as long-sleeved shirts and ties were too _____, and this shirt later became a common fashion item for everyone.

Vocabulary

B Choose the correct word for each definition.

tight	copy	thick	comfortable	youth	cotton	share

1 close fitting, not loose: _____

2 to tell other people about an idea, problem, etc.: _____

3 having a large distance between opposite sides: _____

4 the part of life when one is young: _____

5 feeling physically relaxed and unstressed: _____

6 to do what someone else does because you like them: _____

Reading 1

You've probably seen astronauts working outside their spacecraft on TV. This is called a spacewalk. Astronauts go on spacewalks to build or fix things on their spacecraft. They wear spacesuits during their spacewalks, which can be as long as eight hours. And these spacesuits are more ⁵ than just clothes.

A spacesuit is like _____(A)_____ . It is made up of many different parts, and each part keeps the astronaut safe in space. For example, the backpack on the back of the suit contains oxygen that the astronaut can breathe. ¹⁰ It also has a water bag to drink from. The spacesuit itself has water inside it too. It flows through tubes in the astronaut's underwear. This keeps him or her cool in space! ⓐ Small jets on the suit also help to keep the astronaut safe. ⓑ These help the astronaut fly back if he or she floats away from the spacecraft. ⓒ And space dust makes spacewalks difficult. ⓓ Of course there are systems like a radio, a battery, and ¹⁵ a computer to let the astronaut work in space.

Considering all the parts, it's not surprising that a spacesuit weighs about 280 kg. Thanks to weightlessness in space, however, astronauts can do great work in this heavy suit.

1　**What is the passage mainly about?**

①　the work of astronauts

②　the features of spacesuits

③　the types of spacewalks

④　the systems of a spacecraft

2　**Astronauts work outside the spacecraft to** _____

_____ .

3　**What is the best choice for blank (A)?**

①　a family home

②　a safe message

③　a personal spacecraft

④　a present from the future

4　**Which sentence is NOT needed in the passage?**

①　ⓐ　　　　　　②　ⓑ　　　　　　③　ⓒ　　　　　　④　ⓓ

5　**What is NOT true about spacesuits?**

①　A backpack holds oxygen to breathe in space.

②　A water bag is connected to the spacecraft by tubes.

③　Jets help astronauts to stay close to the spacecraft.

④　A radio, a battery, and a computer are included in a spacesuit.

6　**Write T if the statement is true and F if it's false.**

(1) Spacewalks usually take a couple of days.

(2) Astronauts do not feel the weight of their spacesuits in space.

Before going on a spacewalk, astronauts need more than just a spacesuit —they need lots of training. Here on Earth, there are many trainers who help astronauts get ready for spacewalks.

Ross   I train astronauts _____. Because it is made up of many parts, putting on a spacesuit takes about 45 minutes. I also teach ⁵ them how to use the different tools inside the spacesuit.

Yumin   I teach astronauts everything about spacewalks. Firstly, I train them to be weightless in a special underwater room. Then I show them how to do their work outside a spacecraft. My job is very important.

Tim   My job is managing the technology we use to train astronauts. The ¹⁰ astronauts wear special helmets with computer screens. These allow them to "see" what a spacewalk is like. The astronauts really enjoy this part of the training!

What is the best choice for the blank?

① to correctly wear their spacesuits

② to fix their spacesuits by themselves

③ to keep their balance with a heavy suit

④ to put together the tools for a spacesuit

⑤ to make a safe escape from a spaceship

Summary / Graphic Organizer

A Choose the correct words to fill in the blanks.

| spacewalks | heavy | jets | safe | oxygen |

Reading 1

A spacesuit is an astronaut's most important piece of equipment. It keeps the astronaut _____ while he or she is working outside the spacecraft. Astronauts also need to take _____ sometimes. This would be impossible without a spacesuit. Special features, such as a backpack containing _____ and a water bag, allow the astronauts to breathe and stay hydrated. The spacesuit also has several _____, which help the astronauts get back to the spacecraft.

Vocabulary

B Choose the correct word for each definition.

| float | manage | tool | dust | fix | astronaut | breathe |

1 someone who travels to and works in space: _____

2 something that you use in order to do something: _____

3 to move slowly through the air or stay up in the air: _____

4 to take air into your lungs and let it out again: _____

5 a powder made up of tiny pieces of dirt or other substances: _____

6 to repair something or make it right: _____

Photo credits

www.shutterstock.com

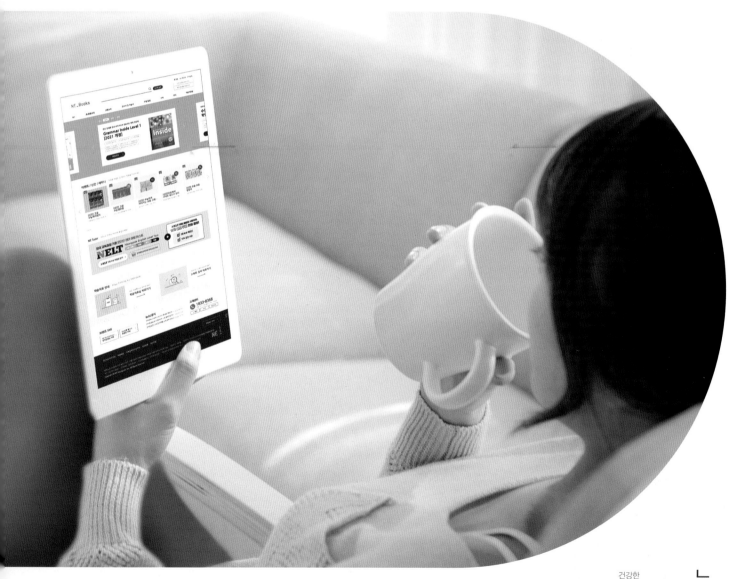

JUNIOR
READING EXPERT

A Theme-Based Reading Course for Young EFL Learners

Level **2**

Word Book

UNIT 01   *Travel*

railway	명 철도, 철길
route	명 노선
ride	명 탐, 타고 감 동 (~을) 타다
journey	명 여행, 여정
cover	동 덮다; (일정 거리를) 가다
passenger	명 승객
share	동 함께 나누다, 공유하다
view	명 경치
get off	내리다
lake	명 호수
known as	~로 알려진
freshwater	형 민물[담수]의
huge	형 거대한
can't wait to-v	어서 빨리 ~하고 싶다
explore	동 탐험하다
ferry	명 여객선
nervous	형 불안한, 긴장한
amazed	형 놀란
order	동 주문하다
purpose	명 목적
stopover	명 (여행 중에) 잠시 들름, 단기 체류
experience	동 경험하다

per	웹 ~당
include	통 포함하다
accommodation	명 숙박
class	명 학급; (품질, 정도에 의한) 등급
insurance	명 보험
booking	명 예약
at least	적어도, 최소한
provide	통 제공하다

UNIT 02 *Teens*

teenage	형 십 대의
teenager	명 십 대
hair loss	탈모
take a shower	샤워를 하다
floor	명 바닥
normal	형 정상적인
lose	통 잃다
hormone	명 호르몬
happen	통 발생하다
fall out	빠지다
nutrition	명 영양
affect	통 영향을 미치다

health	명 건강
healthy	형 건강한
unhealthy	형 건강하지 못한
add	동 더하다
leafy	형 잎이 있는
vegetable	명 채소
meal	명 식사, 끼니
include	동 포함하다
stressed	형 스트레스를 받는
thin	형 얇은 동 (머리가) 숱이 적어지다[빠지다]
hurt	동 다치게 하다
confidence	명 자신감
control	동 조절하다
frequently	부 자주, 종종
tie	명 끈 동 묶다
chemical	형 화학적인
hair treatment	헤어 트리트먼트
weaken	동 약하게 하다
perm	명 파마
prevent	동 막다, 예방하다
wet	형 젖은
grow	동 자라다; 커지다, 늘어나다
sign	명 징후, 조짐
forehead	명 이마

hairline	몡 머리카락 선
bald	혱 대머리의, 머리가 벗겨진
spot	몡 장소, 지점
area	몡 부분
miss	동 놓치다; 없는 것을 알다
furthermore	븜 뿐만 아니라
easily	븜 쉽게
come out	떨어지다, 빠지다
catch	동 잡다; 발견하다
get worse	악화되다
cycle	몡 주기
symptom	몡 증상
manage	동 관리하다
habit	몡 습관

UNIT 03 *Society*

college	몡 대학
personal	혱 개인적인, 사적인
disabled	혱 장애를 가진
brain	몡 뇌
tail	몡 꼬리
unlike	전 ~와 달리

4

up to	~까지
get along with	~와 어울려 지내다
simple	⑱ 간단한, 쉬운
task	⑲ 과제, 일
real	⑱ 실제의
microwave	⑲ 전자레인지
household	⑱ 가정(용)의
several	⑱ 여럿의
perform	⑧ 수행하다
complicated	⑱ 복잡한
graduate	⑧ 졸업하다
talent	⑲ 재능
match	⑧ 조화시키다, 연결시키다
owner	⑲ 주인
so far	지금까지
result	⑲ 결과
fantastic	⑱ 환상적인
give a helping hand	돕다
in addition	게다가
nevertheless	⑭ 그럼에도 불구하고
lifespan	⑲ 수명
lose the use of	~을 사용하지 못하게 되다
accident	⑲ 사고
roommate	⑲ 룸메이트

| compare | 동 비유[비교]하다 |
| close | 형 가까운 |

regular	형 보통의
first of all	우선
invent	동 발명하다, 만들다
create	동 창조하다, 만들다
A.D.	서기 ~ (Anno Domini의 두음어)
count	동 (수를) 세다; 계산하다
realize	동 깨닫다, 이해하다
confusing	형 혼란스러운
take a class	수업을 듣다
grade	명 성적
what if ~?	~하면 어떻게 되는가?
poorly	부 좋지 못하게
space	명 공간, 여백
thanks to	~ 덕분에
clearly	부 명확하게
truly	부 매우, 참으로
letter	명 글자
alphabet	명 알파벳

system	몡 체계
appear	동 나타나다, 나오다
total	형 전체의, 총 ~
thank goodness	~이라 다행이다, 잘 됐다

UNIT 05 Animals

cuckoo	몡 뻐꾸기; 뻐꾹 (소리)
cry	몡 (새, 짐승의) 우는 소리
friendly	형 정다운, 친절한
play a trick on	~을 속이다, ~에게 장난을 하다
trick	몡 속임수, 장난
lay	동 (알 등을) 낳다
nest	몡 둥지
place	동 두다
choose	동 선택하다
similar	형 비슷한, 닮은
unwanted	형 원치 않는, 불필요한
guest	몡 손님
chick	몡 병아리; 새끼 새
hatch	동 부화하다
roll	동 굴리다
take care of	~을 돌보다

behave	⑧ 행동하다
uninvited	⑱ 초대받지 않은
hard-working	⑱ 근면한
host	⑲ 주인
visitor	⑲ 방문객; 손님
welcome	⑧ 환영하다
raise	⑧ 기르다
as soon as	~하자마자
legend	⑲ 전설
major	⑱ 주요한
report	⑧ 보도하다
wood	⑲ (~s) 숲
call out	외치다
in return	답례로, 회답으로
pocket	⑲ 호주머니
role	⑲ 역할
influence	⑲ 영향, 영향력

UNIT 06 *Literature*

be full of	~로 가득 차 있다
fence	⑲ 울타리
punishment	⑲ 벌

punish	동 벌하다
skip	동 건너뛰다, (수업 등을) 빼먹다
sigh	명 한숨
come along	다가오다
mean	형 심술궂은 동 의미하다
tease	동 놀리다, 괴롭히다
pretend to-v	~하는 체하다
beg	동 간청하다
at last	마침내
agree	동 동의하다
long face	침울한 얼굴
joyous	형 즐거운, 신나는
clever	형 영리한
disappointed	형 실망한
embarrassed	형 당황한
best-loved	형 가장 사랑받는
novel	명 소설
especially	부 특히
adventure	명 모험
be based on	~을 토대로 하다
childhood	명 어린 시절
playful	형 장난기 많은
reader	명 독자
run away from	~에서 도망치다

| slave | 몡 노예 |
| serious | 톙 심각한; 진지한 |

UNIT *07* *The Economy*

important	톙 중요한
share	통 공유하다, 나누다
celebration	몡 축하
celebrate	통 축하하다
economy	몡 경제
economic	톙 경제의
offer	통 제공하다
savings account	저축 계좌
account	몡 계좌
spending	몡 지출
spend	통 쓰다
customer	몡 손님, 고객
interest	몡 이자
interest rate	이자율
worry	몡 걱정
save	통 저축하다
savings	몡 저금, 예금
popular	톙 인기 있는

common	혱 흔한
useful	혱 유용한
community bank	지역 은행
remain	통 계속[여전히] ~이다
difficulty	몡 어려움
borrow	통 빌리다
gather	통 모이다
manage	통 관리하다
carefully	튀 조심스럽게, 주의 깊게
decide	통 결정하다
set a goal	목표를 세우다
limit	통 제한하다
make a list	목록을 만들다
application	몡 애플리케이션 (= app)
record	통 기록하다
purchase	몡 구입한 것
follow	통 따르다
tip	몡 조언
confidently	튀 자신 있게
focus on	~에 집중하다
necessary	혱 필요한

UNIT 08 *Science*

fart	몡 방귀 튐 방귀 뀌다
embarrassing	혱 당황하게 하는
embarrassed	혱 당황한
hold in	~을 억제하다[참다]
let out	~을 내다[방출하다]
principal	몡 교장
meal	몡 식사
break down	~을 부수다, 분해하다
belly	몡 배
tiny	혱 아주 작은
bacteria	몡 세균 (bacterium의 복수형)
ammonia	몡 《기체》 암모니아
certain	혱 특정한, 어떤
bean	몡 콩
swallow	튐 삼키다
burp	몡 트림
manner	몡 방법; (~s) 예절
bellyache	몡 복통
cultural	혱 문화적인
lung	몡 폐
breathe	튐 숨쉬다
affect	튐 ~에 영향을 미치다

loud	형 소리가 큰
loudness	명 소리의 크기
depend on	~에 달려 있다, 좌우되다
amount	명 양
smelly	형 냄새 나는, 불쾌한 냄새의 (비교급 smellier)
meat	명 고기, 육류
on the other hand	반면에
be related to	~와 관계가 있다

UNIT 09 Jobs

Antarctic	명 남극, 남극 지방 형 남극의, 남극 지방의
Antarctica	명 남극 대륙
weather scientist	기상학자
weather station	기상 관측소
observe	동 관찰하다
climate	명 기후
dark	형 어두운
rise	동 오르다; (해, 달이) 뜨다
set	동 (해, 달이) 지다
put on	(옷을) 입다
snowsuit	명 눈옷, 방한복
research	명 연구, 조사

fur seal	물개
take measurements	측량[측정]을 하다
measure	동 재다
launch	동 띄우다, 발사하다
weather balloon	기상 관측 기구
temperature	명 기온
equipment	명 장비
treat	명 즐거움을 주는 것, 선물, 대접
aurora	명 오로라
South Pole	남극
icy	형 얼음의, 얼음으로 덮인
continent	명 대륙
midnight	명 자정
pole	명 막대기; 극(極), 극지
polar	형 극지의
rich	형 풍부한
mineral	명 광물
own	동 소유하다
wildlife	명 야생 생물
freezing	형 매우 추운
region	명 지역
carry out	~을 수행하다
follow	동 따르다
strict	형 엄격한

waste	똉 쓰레기
pollution	똉 오염 (물질)
damage	동 훼손하다
environment	똉 환경

UNIT 10 Culture

unique	혱 독특한
mixed	혱 혼합된
culture	똉 문화
tradition	똉 전통
influence	동 영향을 주다 똉 영향(력)
Western	혱 서양의
control	동 지배하다 똉 지배
locate	동 위치를 두다
location	똉 위치
southeast	혱 남동쪽의
coast	똉 해안
as a result	그 결과
diverse	혱 다양한
open-minded	혱 열린 마음의
official language	공용어
come from	~ 출신이다

commonly	⊕ 흔히, 보통
holiday	⊕ 휴일
celebration	⊕ 기념[축하] 행사
Eastern	⊕ 동양의
background	⊕ 배경
blend	⊕ 조합
fact	⊕ 사실
law	⊕ 법
once	⊕ 언젠가, 한때
eating habit	식습관
daily	⊕ 일상의
expensive	⊕ 비싼
dish	⊕ 요리
bun	⊕ 둥근 빵
cheap	⊕ (값이) 싼
heritage	⊕ 유산
fancy	⊕ 값비싼, 고급의

UNIT 11 Issues

education	⊕ 교육
welcome	⊕ 환영하다
store	⊕ 저장하다, 보관하다

receive	⑧ 받다
collect	⑧ 모으다, 수집하다
care about	신경 쓰다
privacy	⑲ 사생활, 프라이버시; 개인 정보
steal	⑧ 훔치다
hacker	⑲ (컴퓨터) 해커
opinion	⑲ 의견
traditional	⑲ 전통적인
method	⑲ 방법
benefit	⑲ 혜택, 이득
policy	⑲ 정책, 방침
protect	⑧ 보호하다
main	⑲ 가장 중요한, 주된
helpful	⑲ 도움이 되는
respect	⑧ 존중[존경]하다
search	⑲ 찾기, 수색; (컴퓨터) 검색
right	⑲ 권리, 권한
recently	⑲ 최근에
issue	⑲ 주제, 쟁점; 문제
remove	⑧ 없애다, 제거하다
request	⑧ 요청하다, 요구하다
threaten	⑧ 위협하다
nature	⑲ 자연; 본질
flow	⑲ 흐름

debate	동 논의[토론]하다
delete	동 삭제하다
support	명 지지, 지원
grow	동 커지다, 증가하다; 자라다
trust	동 신뢰하다, 믿다

UNIT 12 *Food*

cinnamon	명 계피
garlic	명 마늘
ginger	명 생강
saffron	명 사프란
name	동 이름을 대다
spice	명 향신료, 양념
spicy	형 양념 맛이 강한
taste	명 맛
tasty	형 맛있는
add	동 더하다
flavor	명 풍미, 맛 동 맛을 내다
go bad	썩다, 나빠지다
powerful	형 강력한
chemical	명 화학물질
insect	명 곤충

slow	동 늦추다
growth	명 성장
onion	명 양파
oregano	명 오레가노, 꽃박하
be good at	~을 잘하다
recipe	명 조리법
sharp	형 날카로운; 자극적인
produce	동 생산하다
related	형 관련된
valuable	형 귀중한
make up	~을 구성하다
trade	명 무역
actually	부 실제로, 사실
discover	동 발견하다
in search of	~을 찾아서
century	명 세기

UNIT 13 The Environment

imagine	동 상상하다
adventure	명 모험
plan	동 계획하다
local	형 지역의, 현지의

natural	휑 자연의
habitat	명 서식지
ecotourism	명 생태 관광
wonder	명 경이, 놀라움
harm	동 해를 끼치다
participate in	~에 참가하다
activity	명 활동
area	명 지역
tourist	명 관광객
turtle	명 거북
lay	동 (알을) 낳다
regular	휑 규칙적인, 정기적인
interaction	명 상호작용
interact	동 상호작용하다
careful	휑 조심스러운
target	명 목표물
predator	명 포식자
negative	휑 부정적인
effect	명 영향, 효과
approach	명 접근
species	명 종
respond	동 대응하다
contact	명 접촉
endangered	휑 위험에 처한; 멸종 위기에 처한

faithful	⑱ 믿을 수 있는
doubtful	⑱ 의심스러운
concentrate on	~에 집중하다
point out	지적하다, 언급하다
positive	⑱ 긍정적인
opportunity	⑲ 기회
experience	⑧ 경험하다
beauty	⑲ 아름다움
create	⑧ 창조하다
be proud of	~을 자랑으로 여기다
community	⑲ 지역 사회
knowledge	⑲ 지식

UNIT 14 *People*

international	⑱ 국제적인, 세계적인
symbol	⑲ 상징(물)
peace	⑲ 평화
take over	장악하다
forbid	⑧ 금지하다
attend	⑧ 참석하다; (~에) 다니다
comment	⑲ 의견, 논평
shoot	⑧ (총 등을) 쏘다

survive	동 살아남다
refuse	동 거절하다, 거부하다
attack	명 공격
silence	동 침묵시키다 명 침묵
give a speech	연설하다
speech	명 연설
bullet	명 총알
fail	동 실패하다
weakness	명 나약함
fear	명 두려움
hopelessness	명 가망 없음, 절망
strength	명 강인함, 힘
power	명 힘; 권력
courage	명 용기
inspire	동 고무하다; 영감을 주다
national	형 국가의, 국가적인
prize	명 상
encourage	동 격려[고무]하다
effort	명 노력
violence	명 폭력
chore	명 집안일
otherwise	부 그렇지 않으면
fortunately	부 다행스럽게도, 운 좋게도
take place	개최되다, 열리다

representative	명 대표(자)
attention	명 주의 (집중), 주목
honored	형 명예로운; 영광으로 생각하여
darkness	명 어둠, 암흑
realize	동 깨닫다, 알아차리다
importance	명 중요성
value	명 가치
face	동 직면하다
struggle	동 투쟁하다
weapon	명 무기
military	명 군대
resource	명 자원

UNIT 15 Technology

hacker	명 해커
hacking	명 해킹
cybercriminal	명 사이버 범죄자
cybercrime	명 사이버 범죄
break into	침입하다
selfish	형 이기적인
hero	명 영웅
harm	명 해, 피해

steal	동 훔치다
account	명 계좌
detail	명 세부 사항; 정보
society	명 사회
method	명 방법
permission	명 허락, 허가
look for	~을 찾다
security	명 보안
owner	명 주인
in demand	수요가 많은
demand	명 요구, 수요
prevent	동 막다, 방지하다
enter	동 들어가다
direct	형 직접적인
opposite	형 반대의
constant	형 지속적인
threat	명 위협
thankfully	부 고맙게도, 다행스럽게도
lower	동 낮추다
chance	명 가능성
hack	동 해킹하다
first of all	우선
recognize	동 알아보다, 알다
phishing	명 피싱(신용 정보 노출 및 금융 사기 행위)

delete	동 삭제하다
search history	검색 기록
regularly	부 정기[규칙]적으로
gather	동 모으다
enable	동 ~을 할 수 있게 하다
access	동 접근하다
a wide variety of	매우 다양한
device	명 장치, 기구
target	동 목표[표적]로 삼다, 겨냥하다
tip	명 조언
avoid	동 피하다; 방지하다

UNIT 16 *Entertainment*

pepper	명 후추; 피망
vegetable	명 채소
instrument	명 악기
musician	명 음악가, 연주자
healthy	형 건강한
diet	명 식단
drill	명 송곳, 드릴
imagination	명 상상력
audience	명 청중

calm	형 고요한, 평온한
comforting	형 위안을 주는
unique	형 독특한
in addition	게다가
fill	동 채우다
whole	형 전체의, 모든
performance	명 공연
be over	끝나다
wait for	~을 기다리다
please	동 즐겁게 하다
taste	동 맛보다
shape	명 모양
vegetarian	명 채식주의자
prepare	동 준비하다
recorder	명 리코더
practice	명 연습
respect	동 존중하다
organize	동 조직하다, 구성하다

think of	~을 생각하다
ancient	ⓗ 고대의
Egyptian	ⓜ 이집트인 ⓗ 이집트의
including	ⓟ ~을 포함하여
follow	ⓓ 따르다
rule	ⓜ 규칙
fall over	넘어지다
draw	ⓓ (선을 이용하여) 그리다
angle	ⓜ 각도
side	ⓜ 옆(면), 측면
front	ⓜ 정면, 앞
upper	ⓗ 위쪽의
appear	ⓓ 나타나다
realistic	ⓗ 사실적인
describe	ⓓ 묘사하다
various	ⓗ 다양한
be interested in	~에 관심이 있다
artist	ⓜ 화가, 예술가
pure	ⓗ 순수한
goddess	ⓜ 여신
certain	ⓗ 일정한, 특정한

ring	몡 링, 원형 경기장 툉 (종 등이) 울리다
boxing	몡 권투, 복싱
box	툉 권투를 하다
match	몡 경기, 시합
chessboard	몡 체스판
take away	제거하다, 치우다
round	몡 회[라운드]
continue	툉 계속하다
switch	툉 전환하다, 바꾸다
knock out	~을 나가 떨어지게 하다, ~을 의식을 잃게 만들다
run out of	~을 다 써버리다
competition	몡 경쟁; 대회, 시합
spread	툉 퍼지다, 확산되다
strength exercise	근력 운동
strength	몡 힘, 기운
unusual	혱 특이한, 흔치 않은
real	혱 진짜의, 실제의
champion	몡 챔피언, 우승자
rare	혱 드문, 희귀한
originally	뷔 원래, 본래
French	혱 프랑스의, 프랑스인[어]의
cartoonist	몡 만화가

Dutch	혱 네덜란드의, 네덜란드인[어]의
reality	몡 현실

Origins

wool	몡 양모; 모직물
uniform	몡 제복, 군복
cotton	몡 면
undershirt	몡 속셔츠
copy	통 모방하다, 복사하다
army	몡 군대; 육군
navy	몡 해군
include	통 포함하다
consider	통 여기다, 생각하다
underwear	몡 내의, 속옷
shock	통 충격을 주다
outerwear	몡 겉옷
symbol	몡 상징
youth	몡 젊음; 젊은이
rebel	몡 반항
cause	몡 이유, 원인
tight	혱 딱 붙는
development	몡 발달

printing	똉 인쇄(술)
inexpensive	똉 비싸지 않은
canvas	똉 캔버스 천, 화폭
share	똉 공유하다
comfortable	똉 편안한
stylish	똉 멋진
memory	똉 기억
thick	똉 두꺼운
collar	똉 깃, 칼라
invent	똉 발명하다
long-sleeved	똉 긴 소매의
uncomfortable	똉 불편한

UNIT 20 *Space*

astronaut	똉 우주 비행사
spacecraft	똉 우주선
spacewalk	똉 우주 유영
fix	똉 고치다
spacesuit	똉 우주복
be made up of	~으로 이루어지다
space	똉 공간; 우주
backpack	똉 배낭

suit	명 (복장의) 한 벌, 옷
contain	동 ~이 들어있다
oxygen	명 산소
breathe	동 숨 쉬다
flow	동 흐르다
tube	명 관
jet	명 분출; 제트기, 분사 추진기
float	동 뜨다
dust	명 먼지
radio	명 무전기
considering	전 ~을 고려하면
weigh	동 ~의 무게가 나가다
weightlessness	명 무중력 (상태)
weight	명 무게
feature	명 특징, 특색; 기능
personal	형 개인적인
hold	동 수용하다
a couple of	둘의, (몇)개의
train	동 훈련시키다
trainer	명 훈련자, 트레이너
put on	~을 입다
tool	명 도구
underwater	형 수중의
manage	동 관리하다

technology	몡 과학 기술
escape	몡 탈출
spaceship	몡 우주선

JUNIOR
READING EXPERT

A Theme-Based Reading Course for Young EFL Learners

Level 2

Answer Key

NE_ Neungyule

JUNIOR
READING EXPERT

A Theme-Based Reading Course for Young EFL Learners

Answer Key

Level 2

Before Reading   Manchester, U.K., is my dream place! It's because I'm a big fan of Manchester United.

1 ③ **2** ③ **3** ④ **4** ② **5** ③ **6** (1) F (2) F (3) T

해석

엄마 아빠께

저는 시베리아 횡단 철도를 따라 여행 중이에요. 그것은 세계에서 제일 긴 기차 시스템이에요. 몇몇 노선이 있지만, 저는 모스크바에서 블라디보스토크로 가는 노선을 타고 있어요. 이 여정은 약 9,300킬로미터의 거리이고 8일이 걸리는데, 이것은 제가 서쪽에서 동쪽으로 지구의 약 4분의 1을 가는 것을 의미해요!

오늘은 제 여행의 6일째 날이에요. 기차에서 지내는 것은 전혀 지루하지 않아요. 대부분의 승객들은 러시아나 중국에서 온 사람들이에요. 우리는 음식을 같이 나누어 먹고 아름다운 경치를 함께 즐겨요. (이 철도를 건설하는 데는 여러 해가 걸렸어요.) 밤에는 우리의 작은 침대에서 잠을 자죠.

며칠 동안 우리는 시베리아를 통과했어요. 이틀 전에 저는 기차에서 내려 바이칼 호수에 갔어요. '시베리아의 푸른 눈'이라고 알려진 그것은 세계에서 가장 깊고 넓은 담수호예요. 그것을 처음 보았을 때 저는 무슨 말을 해야 할지 몰랐어요. 그것은 정말 거대하고 아름다웠거든요! 저는 그곳에서 도시락을 먹고 차갑고 푸른 물에서 수영을 했지요.

어서 빨리 블라디보스토크를 여행하고 싶어요. 그곳에서 저는 일본으로 가는 여객선을 탈 거예요.

사랑을 담아,
다니엘

어휘

railway 명철도, 철길   route 명노선   ride 명탐. 타고 감 동(~을) 타다   journey 명여행, 여정   cover 동덮다; *(일정 거리를) 가다   passenger 명승객   share 동함께 나누다, 공유하다   view 명경치   get off 내리다   lake 명호수   known as ~로 알려진   freshwater 형민물[담수]의   huge 형거대한   can't wait to-v 어서 빨리 ~하고 싶다   explore 동탐험하다   ferry 명여객선   [문제] nervous 형불안한, 긴장한   amazed 형놀란   order 동주문하다   purpose 명목적   stopover 명(여행 중에) 잠시 들름, 단기 체류

구문 해설

5행   The journey is about 9,300 kilometers long and takes eight days—**that** means (that) I am covering about *one-fourth* of the earth from west to east!

• that: 바로 앞의 내용 (The journey ... eight days)을 가리킴
• one-fourth: 4분의 1 (분수를 표현할 때 분자는 기수로, 분모는 서수로 나타내어 분자 먼저 쓰며, 분자가 2 이상일 때는 분모에 -s를 붙임)

8행   **Being on the train** never *gets* boring.
- Being on the train은 주어로 사용된 동명사구로서 3인칭 단수 취급하므로 동사는 gets를 사용함

15행   When I first saw it, I didn't know **what to say**.
- what to-v: '의문사 + to부정사' 형태로 '무엇을 ～해야 할지'의 의미

Reading 2   p.10

③

해석

시베리아 횡단 철도 여행으로 러시아를 경험하세요!

여행 시간: 11일 (일년 내내)

단체 규모: 10-15인

1인당 가격: 1,800달러

일 정	
1일	모스크바 도착: 호텔에서 전체 미팅
2일	모스크바: 모스크바 자유여행
3 – 5일	기차 여행: 모스크바에서 이르쿠츠크까지
6일	바이칼 호수에 도착하여 2박
7일	바이칼 호수 자유여행
8 – 10일	기차 여행: 이르쿠츠크에서 블라디보스토크까지
11일	블라디보스토크에 도착

포함되는 것	포함되지 않는 것
• 영어를 사용하는 여행 가이드	• 여행 보험
• 조식이 포함된 호텔 숙박	• 러시아 비자
• 이등석 기차표	

예약 및 추가 정보는 sally@fabrussiantour.com으로 이메일을 보내거나 012-555-6789로 전화 주십시오.

어휘

experience ⑧경험하다   per ㉑～당   include ⑧포함하다   accommodation ⑲숙박   class ⑲학급; *(품질·정도에 의한) 등급   insurance ⑲보험   booking ⑲예약   [문제] at least 적어도, 최소한   provide ⑧제공하다

Unit Review   p.11

A   Reading 1   longest, one-fourth, swam, ferry

B   **1** accommodation   **2** view   **3** journey   **4** passenger   **5** include   **6** huge

3

UNIT *02* *Teens*

pp.12-13

Reading 1

Before Reading Yes, I have. When I brush my hair, a lot of it falls out. I think I am experiencing teenage hair loss.

1 (1) ① (2) ③ (3) ② **2** ① **3** I can add foods like fish and leafy vegetables to my meals.
4 ③ **5** ④ **6** (1) F (2) T

해석

십 대 탈모에 대해 자주 묻는 질문들

질문 1: 샤워를 하고 나면, 저는 바닥에서 너무 많은 머리카락을 발견합니다. 이것이 십 대 탈모인가요?

머리카락이 매일 빠지는 것은 정상입니다. 하지만, 요즘 당신의 머리카락이 가늘어지거나 빠지는 일이 더 잦아졌나요? 만약 그렇다면, 그것은 탈모일 수도 있습니다. 십 대 때는 당신의 호르몬 수치가 크게 변합니다. 이런 일이 생기면, 당신의 머리카락이 빠질 수 있습니다. 그런 문제는 의사에게 가서 도움을 요청하세요.

질문 2: 탈모를 예방하는 음식이 있나요?

영양은 우리의 머리카락 건강에 큰 영향을 미치므로, 그렇습니다! 더 건강한 머리카락을 위해 당신의 식사에 생선이나 잎이 많은 채소 같은 음식을 추가해 보세요. 당신의 식사가 충분한 비타민과 미네랄을 포함하지 않을 때, 당신의 머리카락은 건강해 보이지 않고 심지어 빠질 수도 있습니다!

질문 3: 제 얇은 머리카락 때문에 저는 스트레스를 받아요. 제가 머리를 묶거나 파마를 해야 할까요?

탈모가 당신의 자신감을 해칠 수 있다는 것을 알아요. 하지만 스트레스는 탈모의 주요 원인들 중 하나입니다. 그러므로, 그 문제에 대해 생각하기보다는, 당신의 스트레스를 조절하려고 노력하세요. 또한, 머리끈을 자주 사용하거나 화학적인 헤어 트리트먼트를 받는 것은 당신의 머리카락을 약하게 할 수 있습니다.

어휘

teenage 휑십 대의 (teenager 명십 대) hair loss 탈모 take a shower 샤워를 하다 floor 명바닥 normal 휑정상적인 lose 동잃다 hormone 명호르몬 happen 동발생하다 fall out 빠지다 nutrition 명영양 affect 동영향을 미치다 health 명건강 (healthy 휑건강한 unhealthy 휑건강하지 못한) add 동더하다 leafy 휑잎이 있는 vegetable 명채소 meal 명식사, 끼니 include 동포함하다 stressed 휑스트레스를 받는 thin 휑얇은 동(머리가) 숱이 적어지다[빠지다] hurt 동다치게 하다 confidence 명자신감 control 동조절하다 frequently 부자주, 종종 tie 명끈 동묶다 chemical 휑화학적인 hair treatment 헤어 트리트먼트 weaken 동약하게 하다 [문제] perm 명파마 prevent 동막다, 예방하다 wet 휑젖은

구문 해설

3행 **It**'s normal **to lose** hair every day.

· It은 가주어이고, to lose는 진주어로 '~하는 것'의 의미

8행   **Try adding** foods *like* fish and leafy vegetables to your meals for healthier hair.
- try v-ing: 시험 삼아 ~해보다
- like: 《전치사》 ~ 같은

13행   So **rather than** thinking about the problem, *try to control* your stress.
- rather than: ~라기 보다는
- try to-v: ~하기 위해 노력하다

13행   Also, **frequently using hair ties or getting chemical hair treatments** can weaken your hair.

                                                 주어   동사
- frequently using ... hair treatments는 주어로 사용된 동명사구

Reading 2   p.14

②

해석

매일, 당신은 50에서 100개의 머리카락을 잃는다. 그것은 많은 것처럼 들리지만, 오래된 머리카락이 빠질 때는 새로운 머리카락이 자란다. 하지만, 그것이 다시 자라지 않을 때, 당신은 탈모를 겪고 있는 것일 수도 있다. 당신이 이 문제가 있는지 확인하려면, 이러한 징후들을 확인해라. 먼저, 머리카락 선이 전보다 높아져서 이마가 커 보이는지 살펴보아라. 머리카락 선의 얇은 머리카락도 탈모를 나타낼 수 있다. 또 다른 징후는 당신의 머리에 늘어나고 있는 머리카락이 자라지 않는 부분이다. 머리카락이 빠지고 있는 부위를 찾아보아라. 뿐만 아니라, 그것이 쉽게 빠지는지 보기 위해 머리카락을 당기거나 빗어보아라. 당신의 머리카락을 확인하는 것은 당신이 이러한 탈모의 초기 징후들을 발견하는 것을 도울 수 있다. 그러면, 탈모가 더 악화되기 전에 당신은 의사로부터 도움을 받을 수 있다!

어휘

grow ⑧자라다; 커지다, 늘어나다   sign ⑲징후, 조짐   forehead ⑲이마   hairline ⑲머리카락 선   bald ⑱대머리의, 머리가 벗겨진   spot ⑲장소, 지점   area ⑲부분   miss ⑧놓치다; 없는 것을 알다   furthermore ⑨뿐만 아니라   easily ⑨쉽게   come out 떨어지다, 빠지다   catch ⑧잡다; *발견하다   get worse 악화되다   [문제] cycle ⑲주기   symptom ⑲증상   manage ⑧관리하다   habit ⑲습관

구문 해설

3행   **To know** *if you have this problem*, check for these signs.
- To know: 목적을 나타내는 부사적 용법의 to부정사
- if you have this problem은 동사 know의 목적어 역할을 하는 명사절로, if는 '~인지 (아닌지)'의 의미

6행   Look for any areas [**that** are missing hair].
- that 이하는 any areas를 수식하는 주격 관계대명사절

8행   **Checking your hair** can *help you catch* these early signs of hair loss.
- Checking your hair는 주어로 사용된 동명사구
- help + 목적어 + 동사원형: ~가 …하도록 돕다

5

A [Reading 1] hormone, doctor, nutrition, chemical [Reading 2] hairline

B **1** normal **2** weaken **3** bald **4** symptom **5** forehead **6** teenager

[Reading 2 해석]

당신은 머리카락 선이나 머리카락이 빠진 부위, 또는 머리카락이 얼마나 쉽게 빠지는지를 보고 탈모를 확인할 수 있다.

UNIT 03 Society

[Reading 1]   pp.16-17

[Before Reading] I once saw a service dog guide an old lady.

1 ② **2** ② **3** ④ **4** they are only a few months old **5** ② **6** ②

해석

원숭이들은 많은 면에서 사람들과 비슷하다. 사실 그들 중 일부는 심지어 대학에도 간다! 매사추세츠 주의 보스턴에 있는 원숭이 대학은 동물들을 가르쳐 장애를 가진 사람들의 개인 도우미가 되도록 한다.

그들은 몇 가지 이유들로 꼬리감는원숭이(capuchin monkey)를 그들의 '학생'으로 선택했다. 첫째, 그들은 (몸집이) 아주 작지만 큰 뇌를 가지고 있다. 이는 그들을 매우 영리하게 만든다. 그리고 그들은 매우 짧은 꼬리를 가지고 있다. 그래서 다른 원숭이들과 달리 그들은 마치 사람들이 하는 것처럼 그들의 손을 사용한다. 게다가 이 원숭이들은 40년까지 살 수 있고 사람들과 잘 어울릴 수 있다.

이 대학의 원숭이들은 불과 (생후) 몇 개월 밖에 안 되었을 때 훈련을 시작한다. 그들은 음식 가져오기나 물건 집기와 같은 간단한 과제들을 배우기 시작한다. 훈련 센터는 전자레인지, TV 그리고 다른 가정 용품들을 갖춘 실제 집과 비슷하다. 몇 년간의 훈련을 받은 후 원숭이들이 더 복잡한 과제들을 수행할 수 있을 때, 그들은 '졸업한다.' 모든 원숭이는 다른 재능을 갖고 있기 때문에 그들은 자신들의 새 주인들과 신중하게 짝 지어진다. (원숭이들을 훈련시키는 것은 재미있지만 어렵다.) 지금까지 결과는 환상적이었다. 대부분의 주인들은 그들의 원숭이가 도우미일 뿐만 아니라 좋은 친구이기도 하다고 말한다.

어휘

college 명대학 personal 형개인적인, 사적인 disabled 형장애를 가진 brain 명뇌 tail 명꼬리 unlike 전~와 달리 up to ~까지 get along with ~와 어울려 지내다 simple 형간단한, 쉬운 task 명과제, 일 real 형실제의 microwave 명전자레인지 household 형가정(용)의 several 형여럿의 perform 동수행하다 complicated 형복잡한 graduate 동졸업하다 talent 명재능 match 동조화시키다, 연결시키다 owner 명주인 so far 지금까지 result 명결과 fantastic 형환상적인 [문제] give a helping hand 돕다 in addition 게다가 nevertheless 부그럼에도 불구하고 lifespan 명수명

12행   They start to learn simple tasks **such as** bringing food or picking things up.

     • such as 이하는 simple tasks의 구체적인 예들임

15행   **As** every monkey has different talents, they *are* carefully *matched* with their new owners.

     • as: ～하기 때문에

     • are matched: '맞춰지다'라는 뜻으로 'be동사 + 과거분사' 형태의 수동태

18행   Most owners say their monkeys are **not just** helpers **but also** good friends.

     • not just[only] A but also B: A뿐만 아니라 B도

Reading 2   p.18

②

해석

원숭이 도우미와의 생활

Carol E. Lee에 의해 작성됨

베키 톰슨은 사고로 그녀의 팔과 다리를 사용하지 못하게 되었다. 그러나 그녀의 룸메이트인 크리스티가 베키는 할 수 없는 일상의 일들을 도와준다. 크리스티는 22살의 꼬리감는원숭이이다! 그녀는 베키에게 음식과 음료를 갖다주고, 책의 페이지를 넘겨주며, 심지어는 그녀의 이를 닦아 주도록 훈련받았다. 크리스티는 베키의 삶을 엄청나게 변화시켰다. 베키는 그것을 흑백 속에서 사는 것과 컬러 속에서 사는 것 사이의 차이에 비유했다. "크리스티는 단순한 도우미 그 이상이에요. 우리는 서로를 매우 잘 알고 그녀는 내가 어떻게 느끼는지를 항상 알고 있죠. 그녀를 만난 이후로 모든 것이 다 좋아요."라고 그녀는 말했다.

어휘

lose the use of ～을 사용하지 못하게 되다   accident ⑲사고   roommate ⑲룸메이트   compare ⑧비유[비교]하다
[문제] close ⑲가까운

구문 해설

6행   Becky **compared** it **to** the difference [*between* living in black and white *and* living in color].

     • compare A to B: A를 B에 비유[비교]하다

     • between A and B: A와 B 사이에 (있는)

Unit Review   p.19

A   Reading 1   disabled, hands, people, simple, helpers

B   **1** several   **2** disabled   **3** result   **4** compare   **5** complicated   **6** graduate

꼬리감는원숭이들에게 장애를 가진 사람들을 돕도록 가르치는 미국의 한 특별한 '대학'이 있다. 이 종류의 원숭이는 그들이 매우 영리하고 손을 잘 사용하기 때문에 선택되었다. 그들은 또한 사람들과 있는 것을 즐기고 오래 산다. 처음에 그 원숭이들은 간단한 과제들부터 배우기 시작한다. 그들이 좀 더 복잡한 과제들을 할 수 있을 때, 그들은 '졸업하고' 장애를 가진 사람과 함께 살게 된다. 이러한 사람들의 대부분은 그들의 새로운 도우미들과 함께 매우 행복해한다!

UNIT 04 Math

Reading 1

pp.20-21

Before Reading I guess it was made with other numbers a long time ago.

1 ① **2** ③ **3** the idea of zero is difficult to understand **4** ② **5** ③ **6** (1) F (2) T

해석

당신은 아마도 0이 단지 일반적인 숫자라고 생각할지도 모른다. 그러나 그것은 다른 모든 숫자들과 다르다. 우선, 그것은 훨씬 나중에 만들어졌다. 1에서 9의 숫자는 수천 년 전에 만들어졌다. 그러나 숫자 0은 불과 서기 200년에 만들어졌다. (사람들은 그 당시에 숫자를 세기 위해 돌을 사용했다.) 왜 그랬던 것일까? 그것은 0의 개념이 이해하기 어렵기 때문이다.

0을 이해하기 위해서, 당신은 그것이 무(無)와는 다르다는 것을 알아야 한다. 혼란스러운가? 이 예시를 생각해 보라. 당신이 수업을 들으면 당신은 성적을 받는다. 만일 당신이 수업을 듣지 않으면 당신에게는 성적이 없다. 즉 무(無)인 것이다. 그러나 당신이 수업을 듣는데 아주 못한다면 어떻게 되는가? 당신은 0인 성적을 받을 수 있을 것이다.

또한 0은 큰 수를 적는 것을 쉽게 만든다. 0이 있기 전에, 사람들은 일천육(1,006)을 적을 때 '1 6'과 같이 여백을 두었다. 0 덕분에 우리는 일천육을 '1,006'으로 적어서 그것이 106이나 16과 다르다는 것을 명확하게 알 수 있다. 확실히 0은 매우 중요한 숫자이다!

어휘

regular ⑲보통의   first of all 우선   invent ⑧발명하다, 만들다   create ⑧창조하다, 만들다   A.D. 서기 ~ (Anno Domini의 두음어)   count ⑧(수를) 세다; 계산하다   realize ⑧깨닫다, 이해하다   confusing ⑲혼란스러운   take a class 수업을 듣다   grade ⑲성적   what if ~? ~하면 어떻게 되는가?   poorly ⑨좋지 못하게   space ⑲공간, 여백   thanks to ~ 덕분에   clearly ⑨명확하게   truly ⑨매우, 참으로   [문제] letter ⑲글자

구문 해설

2행   First of all, it was invented **much later**.
· much later: '훨씬 나중에'라는 의미로 much가 비교급 later를 수식

6행   It's because the idea of zero is difficult **to understand**.
· to understand: '~하기에'의 의미로 형용사 difficult를 수식하는 부사적 용법의 to부정사

Also, zero **makes it easy** to write large numbers.

가목적어   진목적어

• make + 목적어 + 형용사: ∼을 …하게 만들다

Reading 2

p.22

②

해석

로마 숫자는 알파벳 글자들처럼 생긴 숫자들이다. 이 체계에서는 I이 1 대신 쓰이고, V는 5 대신, X는 10 대신, L은 50 대신, C는 100 대신, D는 500 대신, 그리고 M은 1,000 대신 쓰인다. 그것들은 아라비아 숫자가 만들어질 때까지 유럽 전 지역에서 사용되었다. 오늘날 로마 숫자는 여전히 시계와 달력 같은 것들에 나오기는 하지만, 그것들은 수학에서는 이제 쓰이지 않는다. 그것은 그것들이 길고 어렵기 때문이다. 그리고 읽는 사람은 전체의 숫자를 알기 위해 모든 글자들을 더해야 한다. MMDCCXIII를 예로 들어 보자. 이것은 1,000 + 1,000 + 500 + 100 + 100 + 10 + 1 + 1 + 1, 즉 2,713을 의미한다. 수학 시험에서 로마 숫자를 사용하지 않아서 참 다행이다!

어휘

alphabet 명 알파벳   system 명 체계   appear 동 나타나다, 나오다   total 형 전체의, 총 ∼   thank goodness ∼이라 다행이다, 잘 됐다

구문 해설

1행   In this system, I is used for 1, **V for five, X for 10, L for 50, C for 100, D for 500, and M for 1,000.**

• V for five 이하 6개의 'A for B' 구조의 어구는 각각 for 앞에 is used가 생략되어 있음

Unit Review

p.23

A   Reading 1   special, later, nothing, large, spaces   Reading 2   difficult

B   **1** invent   **2** confusing   **3** letter   **4** appear   **5** grade   **6** total

---

Reading 1 해석

0은 특별한 숫자이다. 그것은 다른 숫자들보다 훨씬 나중에 우리의 숫자 체계에 추가됐다. 그것은 0의 개념이 이해하기 쉽지 않기 때문이다. 그것이 무(無)와는 다르다는 것을 아는 것이 중요하다. 당신이 수업을 듣지 않으면, 당신은 성적을 받지 않는다. 당신은 아무것도 얻지 않는다. 하지만 당신이 수업을 듣고 아주 못한다면, 당신의 성적은 0점이 될 것이다. 0은 또한 큰 숫자들을 쓰는 것을 더 쉽게 만든다. 0이 있기 전에, 사람들은 다른 숫자들 사이에 여백을 사용했다. 하지만 0의 사용으로, 1,006과 같은 숫자들은 이해하기 쉽다!

로마 숫자는 숫자를 나타내는 문자인데, 그것들은 너무 <u>어렵기</u> 때문에 더 이상 수학에서 사용되지 않는다.

UNIT 05 Animals

Reading 1   pp.24-25

Before Reading Yes, I've heard it from the cuckoo clock in my grandma's house.

1 ②   **2** similar in size and color   **3** ②   **4** ①   **5** ④   **6** (1) T (2) F

해석

뻐꾸기는 자신의 이름처럼 '뻐꾹! 뻐꾹!'하는 소리를 내는 새이다. 그 부드러운 울음소리는 정답고 달콤하게 들릴지 모르지만, 뻐꾸기는 그들의 알을 다른 새들의 둥지에 낳아서 다른 새들을 속이고 있다.

어미 뻐꾸기는 20개의 알을 낳고 각각의 알을 서로 다른 둥지에 둔다. 그것은 크기와 색깔이 비슷한 알들이 있는 둥지를 고른다. <u>그런 다음 주인 새가 먹이를 찾아 떠날 때까지 기다린다.</u> 어미 뻐꾸기는 그 새의 둥지로 날아 들어가 자신의 알을 낳고는 빨리 날아가 버린다. 어미 뻐꾸기는 이런 식으로 많은 알을 낳는다.

어미 뻐꾸기만 불청객일 뿐 아니라 새끼 뻐꾸기도 <u>나쁜 손님</u>이다. 새끼 뻐꾸기는 보통 먼저 부화하는데, 그들은 둥지와 먹이를 공유하는 것을 좋아하지 않는다! 새끼 뻐꾸기는 (몸집이) 커서, 그들의 다리를 이용하여 다른 알들과 새끼들을 둥지 밖으로 굴려 내는 것은 그들에게 쉽다. 그 부모들은 그 후에 그들에 대해 잊어버리고, 새끼 뻐꾸기를 돌본다. 새끼 뻐꾸기는 식성이 매우 좋기 때문에 부모 새들은 그것에게 먹이를 주기 위해서 열심히 일한다. 확실히 뻐꾸기는 그들이 행동하는 것보다는 좋은 소리를 낸다!

어휘

cuckoo 명 뻐꾸기; 뻐꾹 (소리)   cry 명 (새·짐승의) 우는 소리   friendly 형 정다운, 친절한   play a trick on ~을 속이다, ~에게 장난을 하다 (trick 명 속임수, 장난)   lay 동 (알 등을) 낳다   nest 명 둥지   place 동 두다   choose 명 선택하다   similar 형 비슷한, 닮은   unwanted 형 원치 않는, 불필요한   guest 명 손님   chick 명 병아리; *새끼 새   hatch 동 부화하다   roll 동 굴리다   take care of ~을 돌보다   behave 동 행동하다   [문제] uninvited 형 초대받지 않은   hard-working 형 근면한   host 명 주인   visitor 명 방문객; 손님   welcome 동 환영하다   raise 동 기르다   as soon as ~하자마자

구문 해설

5행   A mother cuckoo lays 20 eggs, **placing each *one* in a different nest**.
   • placing 이하는 연속동작을 나타내는 분사구문으로 '~하고, 그리고'로 해석함
   • one: an egg를 가리키는 대명사

11행
Not only *is the mother cuckoo* an unwanted guest, **but** the baby cuckoo is **also** a bad
visitor.
　　동사　　　　　주어　　　　　　　　　　보어

- not only A but also B: A뿐만 아니라 B도
- 부정어구(not only)가 문장의 앞에 올 경우에는 주어와 동사를 도치시킴

13행
Cuckoo chicks are big, so it is easy for them to roll the other eggs ... with their legs.
　　　　　　　　　　　　　가주어　　　　의미상 주어　　　진주어

Reading 2　　　　　　　　　　　　　　　　　　　　　　　　　　p.26

③

해석

뻐꾸기는 유럽의 많은 전설에 등장한다. 영국에서는 사람들이 뻐꾸기의 첫 울음소리는 봄을 불러온다고 생각한다. 해마다 주요 신문들은 뻐꾸기의 첫 울음소리를 보도한다. 러시아에서는 사람들은 뻐꾸기가 사람이 얼마나 오랫동안 살 것인지를 알고 있다고 믿는다. 만약 누군가가 숲에서 뻐꾸기 울음소리를 들으면 그 사람은 "뻐꾸기야, 뻐꾸기야, 내가 얼마나 오랫동안 살겠니?"라고 묻는다. 그 사람은 그 새가 '뻐꾹!'하고 답으로 외친 횟수마다 일 년씩 더 살게 될 것이라고 여겨진다. 프랑스에서는 한 전설에 따르면 당신이 주머니에 돈을 갖고 있을 때 봄의 첫 뻐꾸기 울음소리를 듣는 것은 행운이라고 한다. 만일 당신이 그렇게 한다면 당신은 일 년 내내 부유할 것이다!

어휘

legend 명전설　major 형주요한　report 동보도하다　wood 명(~s) 숲　call out 외치다　in return 답례로, 회답으로
pocket 명호주머니　[문제] role 명역할　influence 명영향, 영향력

구문 해설

5행
It is believed that the person will live one more year *for* each time [(when) the bird calls ...].

- it is believed that ~: ~이라고 여겨지다 (it은 가주어, that 이하가 진주어)
- for: ~에 대해[대한]
- the bird 이하는 관계부사절로 앞에 when이 생략되어 있음

Unit Review　　　　　　　　　　　　　　　　　　　　　　　　　　p.27

A　Reading 1　sound, trick, lays, big, feeding　　Reading 2　meaning

B　**1** major　**2** chick　**3** legend　**4** hatch　**5** roll　**6** similar

Reading 1 해석

뻐꾸기는 그것이 내는 정다운 <u>소리</u>에서 이름이 생긴 새이다. 하지만, 뻐꾸기는 다른 새들에게 비겁한 <u>속임수</u>를 쓴다. 어미 뻐꾸기는 다른 새들의 둥지에 알을 <u>낳는다</u>. 다른 새들이 없을 때, 어미 뻐꾸기가 날아와서 각각의 둥지에 알 하나씩을 낳는다. 뻐꾸기의 알이 부화

하면, 새끼 뻐꾸기는 다른 알들과 새끼들을 밀어낼 만큼 충분히 <u>크다</u>. 새끼 뻐꾸기는 많이 먹기 때문에, 다른 새들은 속임수에 넘어가 뻐꾸기의 새끼에게 <u>먹이를 주느라</u> 온종일을 보낸다.

Reading 2 해석

많은 유럽 국가에서 뻐꾸기의 울음소리는 특별한 <u>의미</u>를 가지고 있다.

UNIT 06 *Literature*

Reading 1   pp.28-29

Before Reading I read the book when I was younger. I liked the main character, Tom.

1 ②   **2** She punished him because he skipped school.   **3** ②   **4** ③   **5** ①   **6** ③

해석

토요일 오전이 되었다. 여름은 활기로 가득 차 있었다. 모든 것이 밝고 신선했다. 하지만…

톰은 흰색 페인트 통 하나와 붓을 들고 밖으로 나왔다. 그의 이모는 그에게 학교를 빼먹은 벌로 울타리에 페인트칠을 하라고 화를 내며 말했다. 한숨과 함께 그는 페인트칠을 하기 시작했다.

곧 벤이라는 이름의 소년이 사과를 먹으며 다가왔다. 벤은 항상 톰을 놀려대는 심술궂은 소년이었다. 그는 톰 옆에 서서 말했다. "야, 톰. 너 난처한 상황이구나. 일해야 하나보다!"

톰은 잠시 그를 바라보곤 말했다. "'일'이라니 무슨 뜻이야?"

"그거 일 아니야?" 벤이 물었다.

"천만에! 남자아이가 얼마나 자주 <u>울타리를 칠할</u> 기회를 얻겠어?"

벤은 사과 먹는 것을 멈추고 톰을 바라보았다. 톰은 울타리를 페인트칠하는 매 순간을 아주 즐기는 척했다. 벤은 점점 흥미가 생기기 시작했다. 그가 말했다. "톰, 내가 해볼게."

"아냐, 아냐. 나만 할 수 있어. 이 세상 어느 남자아이도 나만큼 페인트칠을 잘할 수는 없다고."

"제발 내가 해볼게." 벤이 간청히 부탁했다. "네게 내 사과를 줄게!"

마침내 톰은 침울한 표정으로, 하지만 신나는 마음으로 동의했다. 그는 벤이 일을 하기 시작하는 동안에 사과를 먹기 위해 앉았다.

어휘

be full of ~로 가득 차 있다   fence ⑲울타리   punishment ⑲벌 (punish ⑧벌하다)   skip ⑧건너뛰다, (수업 등을) 빼먹다   sigh ⑲한숨   come along 다가오다   mean ⑲심술궂은 ⑧의미하다   tease ⑧놀리다, 괴롭히다   pretend to-v ~하는 체하다   beg ⑧간청하다   at last 마침내   agree ⑧동의하다   long face 침울한 얼굴   joyous ⑲즐거운, 신나는   [문제] clever ⑲영리한   disappointed ⑲실망한   embarrassed ⑲당황한

12

6행　　　Soon a boy [(who was) named Ben] came along, **eating an apple**.

- named 앞에 '주격 관계대명사 + be동사'가 생략되어 있음
- eating an apple은 동시동작을 나타내는 분사구문으로 '～하면서'의 의미임

8행　　　You **must be** in trouble.

- must + 동사원형: ～임에 틀림없다 (강한 추측)

13행　　Ben **stopped eating** the apple and watched Tom, *who pretended to love every minute of painting the fence.*

- stop v-ing: ～하는 것을 멈추다 (*cf.* stop to-v: ～하기 위해 멈추다)
- who 이하는 앞절의 Tom을 부연 설명하는 계속적 용법의 관계대명사절 (who = and Tom)

15행　　**No other boy** in the world can paint **as well as** me.

- no (other) 단수명사 + as + 원급 + as ～: '누구도 ～만큼 …하지 않은'의 의미로 최상급의 의미를 나타냄

Reading 2 　　　　　　　　　　　　　　　　　　　　　　　　　　　p.30

②

해석

마크 트웨인은 미국의 가장 사랑받는 작가들 중 한 명이다. 그의 소설들, 특히 '톰 소여의 모험' (1876)과 '허클베리 핀의 모험' (1885)은 아직도 인기가 아주 많다. '톰 소여의 모험'은 트웨인의 어린 시절 경험을 토대로 하고 있다. 그것은 미시시피강 근처에 사는 한 장난기 많은 소년의 삶에 관한 것이다. (그러나 트웨인은 그의 시대에 미시시피에서 자란 유일하게 유명한 작가는 아니었다.) 우정과 첫사랑, 그리고 모험 이야기는 독자들에게 어린 소년으로 지내는 것의 즐거움을 보여 준다. '허클베리 핀의 모험'은 흑인 노예 짐과 함께, 아버지로부터 도망치는 헉이라고 불린 소년에 관한 것이다. '톰 소여의 모험'보다 좀 더 진지한 이 이야기는 여러 굉장한 모험 중 펼쳐지는 헉과 짐 사이의 우정을 보여 준다.

어휘

best-loved 웹 가장 사랑받는　　novel 몝 소설　　especially 뷔 특히　　adventure 몝 모험　　be based on ～을 토대로 하다　　childhood 몝 어린 시절　　playful 웹 장난기 많은　　reader 몝 독자　　run away from ～에서 도망치다　　slave 몝 노예　　serious 웹 심각한; 진지한

구문 해설

1행　　　Mark Twain is **one of** America's best-loved **writers**.

- one of + 복수명사: ～ 중의 하나

Unit Review

A [Reading 1] punished, tease, fun, tricked   [Reading 2] adventures

B **1** skip **2** beg **3** slave **4** adventure **5** serious **6** tease

Reading 1 해석

화창한 날이었지만, 톰은 학교를 빼먹은 것 때문에 벌을 받고 있었다. 그의 이모는 그가 울타리를 칠해야 한다고 말했다. 그가 페인트칠을 하고 있는 동안, 벤이라는 소년이 다가왔다. 그는 곤경에 처한 톰을 놀리기 시작했다. 하지만 톰은 자신이 벌을 받고 있는 것이 아닌 척했다. 그는 울타리를 칠하는 것이 매우 재미있는 것처럼 행동했다. 곧 벤도 울타리를 칠하고 싶어 했다. 그는 자신이 페인트칠을 하게 해주도록 톰에게 사과 하나를 주었다. 톰은 벤이 자기 일을 하도록 벤을 속였던 것이다!

Reading 2 해석

마크 트웨인은 어린 소년들의 모험에 관한 이야기를 쓴 유명한 미국의 작가이다.

UNIT 07 The Economy

Reading 1

pp.32-33

[Before Reading] I put a skateboard, sneakers, and a new smartphone on my wish list.

1 ③ **2** ① **3** ① **4** offer low interest rates and have people pay to take out money
5 ④ **6** ①

해석

크리스마스는 나눔과 축하를 위한 중요한 시간이다. 그래서 크리스마스가 다가오면, 미국인들은 항상 선물을 사느라 바쁘다.

하지만, 몇 년 동안 불안정한 경제가 이것을 어렵게 만들었다. 그 시기 동안, 사람들은 선물을 사는 데 어려움을 겪었고, 몇몇은 심지어 은행에서 돈을 빌려야 했다! 그래서, 펜실베이니아의 칼라일 신탁회사는 1909년에 크리스마스 클럽을 제공하기 시작했다. 크리스마스 클럽은 휴일 지출을 위한 저축 계좌였다. 은행 고객들은 매주 그 계좌에 약간의 돈을 넣었고, 그들은 오직 크리스마스를 위해 그 돈을 꺼냈다. 시간이 지남에 따라, 은행은 그들의 서비스 이용에 대한 이자, 즉 돈까지 주었다. 그래서 사람들은 돈이 필요하기 전에 걱정 없이 돈을 모을 수 있었다.

경기가 안 좋을 때 크리스마스 클럽이 인기를 끌었지만, 요즘에는 그것이 흔하지 않다. 사람들은 크리스마스 클럽이 유용하지 않다고 말한다. 은행들이 낮은 이자율을 제공하고 사람들이 돈을 빼내기 위해 돈을 내도록 하기 때문이다. 오직 일부 지역 은행들만 여전히 그것들을 제공한다.

하지만 100년이 지난 후에도, 한 가지는 여전히 같다. 우리는 아직도 사랑하는 사람들에게 크리스마스 선물을 주는 것을 좋아한다는 것이다. 그러니 크리스마스를 위해 일찍 돈을 모아두는 게 어떨까?

important ⑧중요한   share ⑧공유하다, 나누다   celebration ⑲축하 (celebrate ⑧축하하다)   economy ⑲경제 (economic ⑧경제의)   offer ⑧제공하다   savings account 저축 계좌 (account ⑲계좌)   spending ⑲지출 (spend ⑧쓰다)   customer ⑲손님, 고객   interest ⑲이자 (interest rate 이자율)   worry ⑲걱정   save ⑧저축하다 (savings ⑲저금, 예금)   popular ⑧인기 있는   common ⑧흔한   useful ⑧유용한   community bank 지역 은행   remain ⑧계속[여전히] ~이다   [문제] difficulty ⑲어려움   borrow ⑧빌리다   gather ⑧모이다

구문 해설

2행   So when Christmas is coming, Americans **are** always **busy with buying** presents.
  • be busy with v-ing: ~하느라 바쁘다

13행   **This is because** banks offer low interest rates and *have people pay* to take out money.
  • this is because ~: 이것이 ~한 이유이다
  • 사역동사(have) + 목적어 + 동사원형: ~가 …하게 하다

Reading 2   p.34

③

해석

  돈은 관리하기 어려울 수 있다. 소비하는 것은 쉽지만 저축하는 것은 그렇게 쉽지 않다. 따라서, 당신의 지출을 신중하게 관리하는 것이 중요하다. 먼저, 당신이 얼마나 저축하고 싶은지 결정하라. 만약 당신이 스스로 목표를 세우면, 당신의 지출을 제한하는 것이 더 쉬워질 것이다. 그런 다음 당신이 살 필요가 있는 물건들의 목록과 당신이 사고 싶은 물건들의 다른 목록을 만들어라. 이렇게 하면 당신은 필요한 물품에 먼저 집중할 수 있다. 마지막으로, 공책 또는 저축 앱을 사용하여 당신이 지출하는 것을 기록하라. 이는 당신이 구입한 것들을 기억하고 당신이 얼마나 저축했는지 알도록 도와줄 것이다. 이러한 쉬운 조언들을 따르면, 당신은 자신 있게 당신의 돈을 관리할 수 있다.

어휘

manage ⑧관리하다   carefully ⑨조심스럽게, 주의 깊게   decide ⑧결정하다   set a goal 목표를 세우다   limit ⑧제한하다   make a list 목록을 만들다   application ⑲애플리케이션 (= app)   record ⑧기록하다   purchase ⑲구입한 것   follow ⑧따르다   tip ⑲조언   confidently ⑨자신 있게   [문제] focus on ~에 집중하다   necessary ⑧필요한

구문 해설

1행   **It's** easy **to spend**, but **it's** not so easy **to save**.
  • 두 개의 It(it)은 각각 가주어이고, to spend와 to save는 진주어로 '~하는 것'의 의미

3행   First, decide on **how much money you want to save**.
  • how much 이하는 간접의문문으로 전치사 on의 목적어 역할을 함

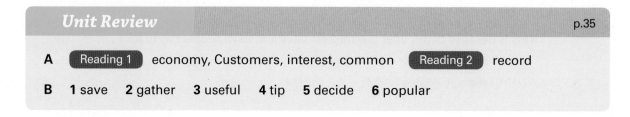

5행   Then make ┌ a list of things [(that) you need to buy]
                │ and
                └ another list of things [(that) you want to buy].

- things 뒤에 목적격 관계대명사 that이 각각 생략되어 있음

7행   This will **help you** ┌ **remember** your purchases
                        │ and
                        └ **see** *how much you've saved.*

- help + 목적어 + 동사원형: ~가 …하도록 돕다
- how much 이하는 간접의문문으로 동사 see의 목적어 역할을 함

Unit Review
p.35

A   `Reading 1`   economy, Customers, interest, common   `Reading 2`   record

B   **1** save   **2** gather   **3** useful   **4** tip   **5** decide   **6** popular

Reading 1 해석

1900년대에, 미국의 경제는 나빴고, 그래서 사람들은 크리스마스 선물을 살 수 없었다. 펜실베니아에 있는 한 신탁회사는 그들을 돕기 위해 크리스마스 클럽을 제공하기 시작했다. 고객들은 크리스마스가 될 때까지 매주 저축 계좌에 돈을 넣을 수 있었다. 그들은 심지어 은행으로부터 이자도 받게 되는 것이었다! 크리스마스가 되면, 그들은 선물을 살 충분한 돈을 갖게 될 것이었다. 하지만 요즘, 크리스마스 클럽은 인기가 없는데, 많은 사람들이 그것들은 쓸모없다고 생각하기 때문이다. 그래서 그것들은 더 이상 은행에서 흔하지 않다.

Reading 2 해석

당신의 지출을 효과적으로 관리하기 위해서는 당신이 얼마나 저축하고 싶은지 결정하고, 필요한 물건을 먼저 사는 데 집중하고, 당신이 구입한 것들을 기록하라.

UNIT *08* *Science*

Before Reading Frankly speaking, yes. I don't think my classmates noticed it though.

1 ① **2** ① **3** (1) ③ (2) ② (3) ① **4** ③ **5** the gas may give you a bellyache **6** ①, ④

해석

케이 박사님께

방귀 뀌는 것은 정말 당황스러워요. 어제 저는 수업 시간에 방귀를 뀌었는데 모두가 그것을 들었어요! 그런데 저는 <u>무엇이 사람들을 방귀 뀌게 만드는지</u> 모르겠어요. 그것에 대해 설명해 주시겠어요? 그리고 방귀를 참는 것이 더 낫나요 아니면 뀌는 것이 더 낫나요?

사이먼

당신의 당황스러운 이야기를 들으니 유감이군요. 하지만 너무 당황해하지 마세요. 어쨌든 누구나 방귀를 뀌니까요. 심지어 당신의 교장 선생님도 방귀를 뀝니다. 영국의 여왕도 그렇고요. 대부분의 사람들은 하루에 14번 방귀를 뀝니다. 그리고 그 이유는 다음과 같지요.

식사를 한 후 당신의 몸은 음식을 분해합니다. 당신의 배 안에는 수십억 개의 아주 작은 세균들이 있어요. 그것들이 음식물을 먹어 치웁니다. 그것들은 먹으면서 가스를 만들어 냅니다. 암모니아와 같은 이 가스들 중 일부는 아주 안 좋은 냄새가 납니다. 특정 음식은 다른 것들보다 더 많은 가스를 만듭니다. 채소와 콩 같은 음식이 많은 가스를 만들죠.

방귀는 또한 공기를 삼킴으로써 생성될 수도 있습니다. 이것은 너무 빨리 먹는다거나 너무 많은 탄산음료를 마실 때 발생할 수 있습니다. 공기의 일부는 트림으로 나옵니다. <u>그리고 일부는 숨을 쉴 때 당신의 폐에서 배출됩니다.</u> 그러나 상당량의 공기는 배로 가서 방귀로 나옵니다.

물론 다른 사람들 앞에서 방귀를 뀌는 것은 좋은 예절이 아닙니다. 그러나 그것들을 참는 것은 주의하세요! 그렇게 할 경우 가스가 당신에게 복통을 일으킬 수도 있으니까 말이죠. 그러니 방귀가 날아가게 두세요!

케이 박사

어휘

fart 명동 방귀 (뀌다)   embarrassing 형 당황하게 하는 (embarrassed 형 당황한)   hold in ~을 억제하다[참다]   let out ~을 내대[방출하다]   principal 명 교장   meal 명 식사   break down ~을 부수다, 분해하다   belly 명 배   tiny 형 아주 작은   bacteria 명 세균 (bacterium의 복수형)   ammonia 명 《기체》 암모니아   certain 형 특정한, 어떤   bean 명 콩   swallow 동 삼키다   burp 명 트림   manner 명 방법; *(~s) 예절   bellyache 명 복통   [문제] cultural 형 문화적인   lung 명 폐   breathe 동 숨쉬다   affect 동 ~에 영향을 미치다

구문 해설

6행   I'm sorry **to hear** your embarrassing story.
   • to hear: '~하다니, ~해서'의 의미로 감정의 원인을 나타내는 부사적 용법의 to부정사

So <u>does</u> <u>the Queen of England.</u>
　　　　　　동사　　　　주어

　　• so + do[does, did] + 주어: (앞에서 한 말에 대해) ~도 역시 그렇다

10행　**Inside your belly** <u>are</u> <u>billions of tiny bacteria.</u>
　　　　　　부사구　　　　동사　　　　주어

　　• 장소의 부사구가 문장의 앞에 위치함에 따라 주어와 동사가 도치됨

Reading 2　　　　　　　　　　　　　　　　　　　　　　　p.38

④

해석

왜 어떤 방귀는 소리가 크고 또 어떤 방귀는 소리가 거의 없는가? 방귀 소리의 크기는 가스의 양에 의해 좌우된다. **(C)** 가스를 더 많이 방출할수록 당신의 방귀 소리는 더 커질 것이다. 그러나 흥미롭게도 방귀의 소리는 그것의 냄새와는 관련이 없다. **(A)** 소리가 큰 방귀가 소리가 안 나는 방귀보다 늘 냄새가 더 많이 난다는 것은 사실이 아니다. 사실 방귀의 냄새는 먹은 음식의 종류에 달려 있다. **(B)** 달걀, 우유, 그리고 육류는 냄새가 아주 고약한 가스를 만들어 낸다. 반면에 콩류와 채소류는 냄새가 없는 대량의 가스를 만들어 낸다.

어휘

loud 휑 소리가 큰 (loudness 몡 소리의 크기)　depend on ~에 달려 있다, 좌우되다　amount 몡 양　smelly 휑 냄새 나는, 불쾌한 냄새의 (비교급 smellier)　meat 몡 고기, 육류　on the other hand 반면에　be related to ~와 관계가 있다

구문 해설

1행　Why are **some** farts loud and **others** quiet?

　　• some ~ others ...: 일부는 ~ 또 다른 일부는 …

8행　**The more** gas you let out, **the louder** your fart will be.

　　• the + 비교급 ~, the + 비교급 …: ~하면 할수록 더 …하다

Unit Review　　　　　　　　　　　　　　　　　　　　p.39

A　Reading 1　reason, normal, bacteria, quickly, bellyache　Reading 2　smell

B　**1** principal　**2** embarrassing　**3** burp　**4** swallow　**5** amount　**6** manners

---

Reading 2 해석

방귀 소리의 크기는 가스의 양에 의해 좌우되는 반면, 방귀의 냄새는 당신이 무엇을 먹는지에 의해 좌우된다.

Reading 1

pp.40-41

Before Reading Maybe I could have some fun with penguins!

1 ③ **2** how the climate will change in the future **3** ② **4** ② **5** ④ **6** (1) F (2) T (3) F

해석

남극에 오신 걸 환영합니다! 제 이름은 그레그이고 저는 기상학자입니다. 연간 6개월 동안 저의 팀과 저는 이곳 기상 관측소에서 생활합니다. 우리의 임무는 남극의 날씨를 관찰하고 기후가 미래에 어떻게 바뀔지 연구하기 위해 그 정보를 이용하는 것입니다.

저의 하루는 오전 7시에 시작됩니다. 제가 깨어날 때는 날이 아직 어둡습니다. 사실, 이곳은 겨울에 해가 전혀 뜨지 않습니다. 그리고 여름에는 해가 전혀 지지 않습니다. 제 방한복을 입은 후에 저는 연구소로 걸어갑니다. 그것은 바닷가 옆에 있어서 저는 종종 물개들과 펭귄들을 봅니다. 저는 그곳에서 오후 세 시까지 세 시간마다 측정을 합니다. 제가 가장 좋아하는 일은 기상 관측 기구를 띄우는 겁니다. 저는 그것을 헬륨으로 채워서 하늘로 보냅니다. (남극의 기온은 영하 35도까지 내려갑니다.) 기상 관측 기구에는 특수 장비가 들어 있습니다. 그것은 대기의 기온과 풍속을 측정합니다. 저녁에 우리는 책을 읽거나, 이야기하거나, 영화를 봅니다. 그러나 어떤 밤에는 특별한 선물을 받습니다. 바로 밤하늘에 여러 색을 가진 아름다운 빛인 오로라입니다.

저는 남극이 지구상에서 가장 아름다운 장소라고 생각합니다. 그리고 얼음으로 덮인 남극 대륙에서 제 직업은 절대로 지루해지지 않습니다.

어휘

Antarctic 몡 혱남극(의), 남극 지방(의) (Antarctica 몡남극 대륙) weather scientist 기상학자 (weather station 기상 관측소) observe 동관찰하다 climate 몡기후 dark 혱어두운 rise 동오르다; *(해·달이) 뜨다 (↔ set 동(해·달이) 지다) put on (옷을) 입다 snowsuit 몡눈옷, 방한복 research 몡연구, 조사 fur seal 물개 take measurements 측량[측정]을 하다 (measure 동재다) launch 동띄우다, 발사하다 weather balloon 기상 관측 기구 temperature 몡기온 equipment 몡장비 treat 몡즐거움을 주는 것, 선물, 대접 aurora 몡오로라 South Pole 남극 icy 혱얼음의, 얼음으로 덮인 continent 몡대륙 [문제] midnight 몡자정

구문 해설

3행 Our job is to ┌ **observe** the Antarctic weather
and
└ **use** that information *to study* **how the climate will change** ...

- to observe와 (to) use는 동사 is의 보어로 쓰인 to부정사로 '~하는 것'의 의미
- to study: 목적을 나타내는 부사적 용법의 to부정사
- how 이하는 study의 목적어절로 쓰인 간접의문문

10행 I take measurements there **every three hours** until three p.m.

- every + 기수 + 복수명사: ~ 간격으로, 마다

15행   However, on some nights we get a special treat: the auroras—beautiful colored lights in the night sky.

• 콜론(:) 이하는 a special treat의 구체적 내용

Reading 2   p.42

③

해석

북극과 남극은 조용하고 아름다운 곳이다. 그곳들은 너무나 추워서 사람들과 동물들이 거의 살지 않는다. 두 극지방 모두 천연 석유와 가스 및 광물이 풍부하다. 그렇다면 누가 그곳을 소유하고 있을까? 사실, 어느 나라도 극지방을 소유할 수 없다. 그 대신, 국가들은 그곳에 연구 기지를 가질 수 있다. 오늘날 총 30개의 국가가 극지방에 연구 기지를 가지고 있다. 수천 명의 과학자들이 이 매우 추운 지역들에서 날씨와 야생 생물을 연구한다. 그들은 원하는 연구는 무엇이든지 할 수 있지만, 모두 다 한 가지 엄격한 규정을 따라야 한다. 그들은 어떤 쓰레기 또는 오염물질도 남겨서는 안 되며 아름다운 극지방의 환경을 훼손하는 어떤 일도 해서는 안 된다는 것이다.

어휘

pole 똉막대기; *극(極), 극지 (polar 휑극지의) rich 휑풍부한 mineral 똉광물 own 퇭소유하다 wildlife 똉야생 생물 freezing 휑매우 추운 region 똉지역 carry out ~을 수행하다 follow 퇭따르다 strict 휑엄격한 waste 똉쓰레기 pollution 똉오염 (물질) damage 퇭훼손하다 environment 똉환경

구문 해설

1행   They are **so cold that** few people or animals live there.

• so ~ that ...: 너무 ~하여 …하다

Unit Review   p.43

A Reading 1 change, snowsuit, measurements, balloon   Reading 2 carry out
B **1** launch **2** wildlife **3** observe **4** treat **5** continent **6** temperature

Reading 1 해석

그레그는 남극에 있는 기상 관측소에서 일하는 과학자이다. 그의 주된 임무는 날씨를 관찰하고 기후 변화를 연구하는 것이다. 그는 오전 7시에 일어나서 그의 방한복을 입는다. 그러고 나서 그는 연구소로 걸어간다. 그곳에서, 그는 오후 3시까지 측정을 한다. 그는 대기 온도와 풍속을 확인하기 위해 기상 관측 기구를 하늘로 보낸다. 그는 밤에는 책을 읽고 그의 팀원들과 이야기를 나눈다. 때때로 그는 오로라의 아름다운 빛이라는 특별한 선물을 받는다.

Reading 2 해석

어느 나라도 북극이나 남극을 소유하지 않지만, 많은 나라들이 이 장소들에서 연구를 수행한다.

Before Reading   Hong Kong is famous for delicious food and great views at night.

1 ③   **2** ④   **3** ②   **4** ③, ④   **5** ②   **6** (1) F (2) T

해석

홍콩은 혼합된 문화를 가진 독특한 장소이다. 그곳은 중국의 특별 지역이기 때문에 많은 중국 전통들을 따른다. 하지만 그곳은 또한 서양 문화의 영향을 받는다. 이는 홍콩이 1841년부터 1997년까지 영국의 지배를 받았기 때문이다. (홍콩은 중국의 남동쪽 해안에 위치해 있다.) 그 결과 홍콩의 문화는 다양하고, 사람들은 열린 마음을 가지고 있다.

홍콩이 영국의 지배 아래에 있었을 때, 유일한 공용어는 영어였다. 하지만, 홍콩의 많은 사람들은 중국의 광둥 지방 출신이다. 그래서 그들의 언어 또한 흔히 사용되었다. 그리고 요즘에는 중국어와 영어 둘 다 공용어로 사용된다.

홍콩은 또한 중국과 서양의 휴일을 모두 기념한다. 예를 들어, 음력 설과 중추절 같은 중국의 명절은 홍콩 사람들에게 큰 기념일이다. 하지만 그들은 부활절과 크리스마스 같은 서양 휴일도 기념한다.

그곳의 역사 때문에, 홍콩은 동양과 서양의 전통을 둘 다 따른다. 그곳은 특별한 문화를 가지고 있고, 사람들은 많은 다른 배경에서 온다.

어휘

unique 휑독특한   mixed 휑혼합된   culture 몡문화   tradition 몡전통   influence 됭영향을 주다 몡영향(력)
Western 휑서양의   control 됭지배하다 몡지배   locate 됭위치를 두다 (location 몡위치)   southeast 휑남동쪽의
coast 몡해안   as a result 그 결과   diverse 휑다양한   open-minded 휑열린 마음의   official language 공용어
come from ~ 출신이다   commonly 븀흔히, 보통   holiday 몡휴일   celebration 몡기념[축하] 행사   Eastern 휑동
양의   background 몡배경   [문제] blend 몡조합   fact 몡사실   law 휑법

구문 해설

4행   This is because Hong Kong **was controlled** by England *from* 1841 *to* 1997.

• was controlled: '지배를 받았다'라는 뜻으로 'be동사 + 과거분사' 형태의 수동태

• from A to B: A에서 B까지

11행   And nowadays, **both** Chinese **and** English *are used as* official languages.

• both A and B: A와 B 둘 다

• be used as: ~로 사용되다

13행   For example, <u>Chinese holidays **such as** Lunar New Year and the Mid-Autumn Festival</u> <u>are</u>
                           주어   동사

big celebrations for the people of Hong Kong.

• such as 이하는 Chinese holidays의 구체적인 예들임

④

홍콩의 음식은 종종 그곳의 독특한 문화를 보여 준다. 홍콩 스타일의 카페인 차찬텡이 이것의 좋은 예이다. 한때 영국의 지배 아래에 있었기 때문에, 홍콩 사람들은 그들의 일상생활에 서양식 식습관을 추가하기 시작했다. 그러나 일반 근로자들에게 서양식 식당은 너무 비쌌다. 그래서 차찬텡이 만들어졌다. 서양에서는 케이크를 먹는 것과 우유를 넣은 차를 마시는 것이 일반적이었다. 차찬텡은 밀크티, 파인애플빵, 그리고 에그타르트와 같은 음료와 요리를 만들기 위해 이 아이디어들을 이용했다. 음식이 매우 저렴했기 때문에, 이 카페들은 점점 더 인기가 많아졌다. 이제, 어떤 요리들은 심지어 홍콩 문화유산의 중요한 부분으로 여겨진다.

once (부)언젠가, 한때   eating habit 식습관   daily (형)일상의   expensive (형)비싼   dish (명)요리   bun (명)둥근 빵
cheap (형)(값이) 싼   heritage (명)유산   [문제] fancy (형)값비싼, 고급의

9행   As the food was so cheap, these cafés became **more and more popular**.
        · 비교급 + and + 비교급: 점점 더 ∼한

10행   Now, some dishes **are** even **seen as** important parts of Hong Kong's cultural heritage.
        · A is seen as B: A가 B로 여겨지다 ('A를 B로 여기다'란 뜻의 'see A as B'의 수동태임)

Unit Review   p.47

A   [Reading 1] controlled, English, Chinese, celebrated   [Reading 2] dishes
B   1 fancy   2 location   3 coast   4 mixed   5 unique   6 influence

차찬텡에서 판매되는 요리들은 서양의 식습관에서 영감을 받았고, 그것들은 홍콩의 문화에 중요하다.

UNIT 11 Issues

Reading 1   pp.48-49

Before Reading   I saw teachers using some apps to manage the class and our homework.

1 ③   **2** ①   **3** ②   **4** ④   **5** the most important thing is students' privacy   **6** ②

해석

많은 학생들이 요즘 학교에서 공부하기 위해 교육용 앱과 웹사이트를 사용한다. 어떤 사람들은 이러한 신기술들을 환영한다. 하지만 다른 사람들은 그 신기술들에 저장된 학생 데이터가 안전하지 않다고 걱정한다.

제이슨: 저는 교육용 앱과 웹사이트가 학교에서 사용되어야 한다고 생각합니다. 주된 이유는 그것들이 교사들에게 도움이 된다는 것입니다. 그것들은 교사들이 학생들이 어떤 것에서 더 많은 도움을 필요로 하는지 알게 해줄 수 있습니다. 그것들은 또한 교사들이 더 나은 학습 계획안을 세우도록 도와줄 수 있습니다. 결국, 이것은 학생들이 더 나은 교육을 받도록 도와줄 것입니다.

토마스: 저는 이러한 신기술들이 학교에서 사용되어서는 안 된다고 생각합니다. 수집된 데이터는 학교에 보관되지 않기 때문에, 안전하지 않습니다. 이러한 프로그램들을 만드는 회사들은 학생들의 개인 정보에 신경 쓰지 않습니다. 실제로, 학생 데이터는 이미 해커들에 의해 도난당한 적이 있습니다.

리사: 제 의견으로는, 학교는 가능한 한 많은 신기술을 사용해야 합니다. 그들이 전통적인 교수법만 사용한다면, 학생들은 지루해할 것입니다. 그리고 학생들이 흥미가 없다면, 그들은 배우지 않을 것입니다.

안젤라: 이러한 신기술들은 정말 많은 이점이 있습니다. 하지만 가장 중요한 것은 학생들의 개인 정보입니다. 저는 학생 데이터를 보호하기 위해 몇 가지 정책들이 만들어져야 한다고 생각합니다.

어휘

education 圐교육   welcome 圐환영하다   store 圐저장하다, 보관하다   receive 圐받다   collect 圐모으다, 수집하다   care about 신경 쓰다   privacy 圐사생활, 프라이버시; *개인 정보   steal 圐훔치다   hacker 圐(컴퓨터) 해커   opinion 圐의견   traditional 圐전통적인   method 圐방법   benefit 圐혜택, 이득   policy 圐정책, 방침   protect 圐보호하다   [문제] main 圐가장 중요한, 주된   helpful 圐도움이 되는   respect 圐존중[존경]하다

구문 해설

6행   They can **let teachers know** *what students need more help in*.
- 사역동사(let) + 목적어 + 동사원형: ~가 …하게 하다
- what 이하는 know의 목적어 역할을 하는 간접의문문

12행   The companies [**that** create these programs] don't care about students' privacy.
              주어   동사
- that: The companies를 선행사로 하는 주격 관계대명사

13행   In fact, student data **has** already **been stolen** by hackers.
- has been stolen: '경험'을 나타내는 현재완료 수동태

④

해석

웹 검색 엔진은 데이터를 찾고 저장하는 데 정말 유익하다. 이것은 인터넷을 매우 도움이 되게 만들지만, 만약 당신이 자신에 대한 정보를 삭제하고 싶어 한다면 매우 나쁘다. 이것이 '잊힐 권리' 법이 최근에 문제가 된 이유이다. 이 법은 누군가 정보 삭제를 요청하면, 인터넷 회사들이 데이터를 삭제하게 할 것이다. 이것은 여러분의 개인 정보를 보호하도록 도와줄 것이지만, 일부 사람들은 그것이 인터넷의 개방성과 정보의 자유로운 흐름을 위협할 것이라고 말한다. 몇몇 나라들은 이미 '잊힐 권리'를 법으로 받아들인 반면에, 다른 나라들은 여전히 그 주제에 대해 논의 중이다. 그러나 일부 인터넷 회사들은 당신이 요청하더라도 당신의 데이터를 삭제할 필요가 없기 때문에 '잊힐 권리'에 대한 지지는 증가하고 있다.

어휘

search 몡찾기, 수색; *(컴퓨터) 검색   right 몡권리, 권한   recently 튄최근에   issue 몡주제, 쟁점; *문제   remove 동없애다, 제거하다   request 동요청하다, 요구하다   threaten 동위협하다   nature 몡자연; *본질   flow 몡흐름   debate 동논의[토론]하다   delete 동삭제하다   support 몡지지, 지원   grow 동커지다, 증가하다; 자라다   [문제] trust 동신뢰하다, 믿다

구문 해설

2행   This **makes the internet** very **helpful**, ...
       • make + 목적어 + 형용사: ~을 …하게 만들다

3행   **That's why** the "right to be forgotten" law has recently become an issue.
       • that's why ~: 그것이 ~한 이유이다, 그래서 ~하다 (why는 선행사를 포함하는 관계부사)

4행   This law will **make internet companies remove** data if someone requests it.
       • 사역동사(make) + 목적어 + 동사원형: ~가 …하게 하다

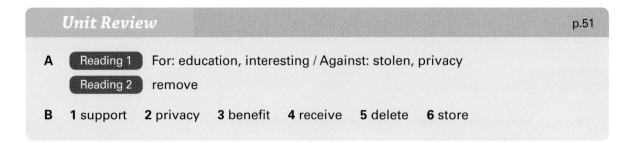

Unit Review   p.51

A   Reading 1   For: education, interesting / Against: stolen, privacy
    Reading 2   remove

B   **1** support   **2** privacy   **3** benefit   **4** receive   **5** delete   **6** store

Reading 2 해석

'잊힐 권리'는 몇몇 인터넷 회사에게 사용자의 온라인 데이터를 삭제하라고 강요하고 있지만, 일부는 그것이 인터넷을 덜 개방적이게 만들 것이라고 우려한다.

Reading 1   pp.52-53

Before Reading I like black pepper the most. It makes food spicier and tastier!

1 ② **2** unique smells and tastes **3** ③ **4** ④ **5** ① **6** ②

해석

계피, 마늘, 생강, 그리고 사프란… 당신은 아마도 몇 가지 향신료의 이름을 댈 수 있을 것이다. 향신료는 잎, 꽃, 또는 열매와 같은 식물의 일부분이다. 그것에는 독특한 냄새와 맛이 있어서 사람들은 음식에 맛을 더하기 위해 그것을 사용한다.

그런데 향신료는 또한 더 중요한 일을 한다. 향신료는 음식이 상하는 것을 막아 준다. 이것은 향신료에 강력한 화학물질이 있기 때문이다. 이 화학물질들은 그 향신료 식물을 세균과 곤충 및 굶주린 동물들로부터 보호한다. 우리가 음식에 향신료를 사용할 때 그 동일한 화학물질들은 같은 작용을 한다. 바로 그것들이 음식을 상하게 하는 위험한 세균들을 죽이거나 그 성장을 늦추는 것이다. 특히 마늘, 양파와 오레가노가 세균들을 죽이는 데에 효과적이다.

그러므로 음식이 빨리 상하는 날씨가 더운 곳의 음식이 더 강한 맛을 내는 것은 놀라운 일이 아니다. 에티오피아와 인도 같은 나라들은 세계의 그 어떤 나라보다도 더 많은 향신료를 사용한다. 그들은 대체로 각 요리법마다 약 6가지의 향신료를 사용한다. 그러나 보통 날씨가 추운 북유럽에서는 많은 요리법들이 향신료를 전혀 쓰지 않는다.

더운 나라의 사람들은 향신료를 사랑할 만한 충분한 이유를 가지고 있다. 향신료가 그들의 음식을 더 맛있고 <u>더 안전하게</u> 만든다!

어휘

cinnamon 명 계피 garlic 명 마늘 ginger 명 생강 saffron 명 사프란 name 동 이름을 대다 spice 명 향신료, 양념 (spicy 형 양념 맛이 강한) taste 명 맛 (tasty 형 맛있는) add 동 더하다 flavor 명 풍미, 맛 동 맛을 내다 go bad 썩다, 나빠지다 powerful 형 강력한 chemical 명 화학물질 insect 명 곤충 slow 동 늦추다 growth 명 성장 onion 명 양파 oregano 명 오레가노, 꽃박하 be good at ~을 잘하다 recipe 명 조리법 [문제] sharp 형 날카로운; *자극적인 produce 동 생산하다 related 형 관련된

구문 해설

5행   Spices **keep food from going** bad.
       • keep + 목적어 + from v-ing: ~가 …하는 것을 막다

12행   …, **it's** not surprising **that** foods are spicier in places with hot weather, *where foods go bad quickly.*
       • it은 가주어, that 이하는 진주어임
       • where 이하는 places with hot weather를 부연 설명하는 계속적 용법의 관계부사절

13행   Countries like Ethiopia and India use **more** spices **than any other country** in the world.
       • 비교급 + than any other + 단수명사: 다른 어떤 ~보다 더 …한 (최상급의 의미)

⑤

해석

후추는 오늘날 매우 흔한 향신료이다. 그러나 과거에는 그것이 아주 귀중하여 심지어 돈으로 사용되기도 했다. **(C)** 당시 후추 1그램은 금 1그램에 판매되었다. 그래서 15세기에 유럽인들은 인도로 가는 가장 가까운 길을 찾으려고 애썼는데, 그곳에서 후추가 생산되었기 때문이다. **(B)** 그리고 이러한 향신료 탐색은 실제로 세계사를 바꿨다. 크리스토퍼 콜럼버스가 아메리카 대륙을 발견하도록 이끈 것이 바로 후추였다. 그는 새로운 땅이 아니라 인도로 가는 새로운 길을 찾아 그의 여행을 시작한 것이었다. **(A)** 나중에 후추는 누구나 살 수 있을 만큼 충분히 값이 싸졌다. 그러나 그것은 여전히 중요하여 세계 향신료 무역의 5분의 1을 차지한다.

어휘

valuable ⑲귀중한   make up ~을 구성하다   trade ⑲무역   actually ⑲실제로, 사실   discover ⑧발견하다   in search of ~을 찾아서   century ⑲세기

구문 해설

3행   Later, pepper became **cheap enough for everyone to buy**.
- 형용사 + enough for A to-v: A가 ~할 만큼 충분히 …한 (for everyone은 to buy의 의미상 주어)

6행   **It was** pepper **that** led Christopher Columbus to discovering America.
- it is ~ that …: …인 것은 바로 ~이다 (강조구문)

Unit Review   p.55

A   Reading 1   plants, unique, bacteria, hotter   Reading 2   value
B   **1** growth   **2** insect   **3** trade   **4** discover   **5** flavor   **6** sharp

Reading 1 해석

향신료는 잎, 꽃, 그리고 열매와 같은 식물의 일부로 만들어진다. 그것은 음식에 독특한 향과 맛을 더하는 데 사용된다. 하지만 향신료는 또한 그 밖의 역할도 한다. 향신료에 들어있는 화학물질은 음식을 상하게 하는 세균들을 죽인다. 따라서, 향신료는 음식이 더 오래 지속되도록 도울 수 있다. 이것이 세계의 더 더운 지역의 국가들이 보통 그들의 음식에 더 많은 향신료를 넣는 이유이다.

Reading 2 해석

15세기에 후추의 높은 가치는 콜럼버스가 아메리카 대륙을 발견했던 이유이지만, 오늘날 후추는 흔하고 값싼 향신료이다.

pp.56-57

Before Reading I think it's good because I can directly see how animals live in nature.

1 ③   **2** ③   **3** ④   **4** too many tourists came to watch them   **5** ④   **6** ①, ④

해석

케냐의 호텔에서 일어나는 것을 상상해 보라. 당신에게는 모험으로 가득 찬 하루가 계획되어 있다. 가이드는 당신이 코끼리, 사자, 그리고 얼룩말을 포함한 현지 동물들을 그들의 자연 서식지에서 볼 수 있게 데려갈 것이다!

이것은 환경에 해를 끼치지 않고 자연계의 경이를 바로 가까이에서 보는 방법인 생태 관광의 한 예이다. 매년, 수백만 명의 사람들이 생태 관광에 참가한다. 많은 사람들은 이러한 활동들이 이 지역들을 보호하는 것을 돕는다고 말한다. 하지만, 일부 연구원들은 <u>의문을 가진다</u>. 그들은 관광객들이 동물들에게 문제를 일으키고 있다고 생각한다. 예를 들면, 코스타리카의 바다거북들은 최근에 그들의 알을 낳는 것에 문제를 겪었는데 왜냐하면 너무 많은 관광객들이 그들을 보러 왔기 때문이다.

또한, 친절한 인간과의 규칙적인 상호작용은 동물들이 덜 조심스럽게 만들지도 모른다. 이것은 그것들이 포식자에게 더 쉬운 목표물이 되도록 만들 수 있다. 이러한 부정적인 영향 때문에, 우리는 생태 관광에 신중한 접근을 해야 한다. 우리는 어떻게 각각 다른 종들이 인간 방문객들에 반응할지를 알아야 한다. 그리고 우리는 인간의 접촉이 동물들을 어떤 식으로든 위험에 빠뜨리지 않도록 확실히 해야 한다.

어휘

imagine 통 상상하다   adventure 명 모험   plan 통 계획하다   local 형 지역의, 현지의   natural 형 자연의   habitat 명 서식지   ecotourism 명 생태 관광   wonder 명 경이, 놀라움   harm 통 해를 끼치다   participate in ～에 참가하다   activity 명 활동   area 명 지역   tourist 명 관광객   turtle 명 거북   lay 통 (알을) 낳다   regular 형 규칙적인, 정기적인   interaction 명 상호작용 (interact 통 상호작용하다)   careful 형 조심스러운   target 명 목표물   predator 명 포식자   negative 형 부정적인   effect 명 영향, 효과   approach 명 접근   species 명 종   respond 통 대응하다   contact 명 접촉   [문제] endangered 형 위험에 처한; 멸종 위기에 처한   faithful 형 믿을 수 있는   doubtful 형 의심스러운   concentrate on ～에 집중하다

구문 해설

8행   Many people say **that these activities *help protect* these areas**.
   • that 이하는 say의 목적어로 사용된 명사절
   • help + (to) 동사원형: ～하도록 돕다, ～에 도움이 되다

14행   This could **make them easier targets** for predators.
   • make + 목적어 + 목적보어(명사): ～을 …로 만들다

16행   And we must **make sure** that human contact does not *put* animals *at risk* in any way.
   • make sure: 반드시 ～하도록 하다, ～을 확실히 하다

• put ~ at risk: ~을 위험에 처하게 하다

Reading 2   p.58

⑤

해석

어떤 사람들은 생태 관광의 부정적인 영향을 지적할지도 모르지만, 그것은 많은 이점 또한 지니고 있다. 그것의 가장 긍정적인 영향의 일부는 환경에 있다. 생태 관광은 사람들이 자연을 존중하도록 돕는다. 이것은 그들이 야생 동물과 자연 지역을 보호하는 것에 좀 더 관심을 갖게 만든다. 방문객들에게 있어, 생태 관광은 좋은 기회를 제공한다. 그들은 자연 세계의 아름다움을 경험할 수 있다. 그들은 또한 새로운 사람들을 만나고 그들의 문화에 대해 배울 수 있다. 생태 관광은 또한 현지 사람들을 위한 일자리를 마련해 준다. <u>그들은 가이드로 일할 수 있고 그들의 지식을 방문객들과 공유할 수 있다.</u> 이런 종류의 일은 또한 그들이 자신의 지역 사회를 자랑스러워하도록 도울 수 있다.

어휘

point out 지적하다, 언급하다   positive ⓗ긍정적인   opportunity ⓜ기회   experience ⓥ경험하다   beauty ⓜ아름다움   create ⓥ창조하다   be proud of ~을 자랑으로 여기다   community ⓜ지역 사회   [문제] knowledge ⓜ지식

구문 해설

3행 **Some of its most positive effects** *are* on the environment.
   • 'some of + 명사'가 주어로 쓰인 경우 of 뒤의 명사의 수에 동사의 수를 일치시키며, 여기서 effects가 복수이므로, 복수형 동사 are가 쓰임

5행 This **makes them care** more about *protecting* wildlife and natural areas.
   • 사역동사(make) + 목적어 + 동사원형: ~가 …하도록 하다[만들다]
   • protecting 이하는 전치사 about의 목적어로 쓰인 동명사구

Unit Review   p.59

A Reading 1 habitats, problems, interact, careful   Reading 2 respect
B 1 negative 2 area 3 predator 4 harm 5 positive 6 doubtful

Reading 1 해석

생태 관광은 환경을 보전하면서 사람들이 자연의 경이를 볼 수 있게 한다. 많은 사람들은 이것이 동물들의 자연 서식지를 보호하는 것을 돕는다고 말하지만, 다른 사람들은 관광객들이 문제들을 일으킨다고 말한다. 예를 들어, 코스타리카의 바다거북은 최근에 알을 낳을 수 없었는데, 너무 많은 관광객들이 그것들을 지켜보기 위해 왔기 때문이다. 또한, 친절한 인간과 정기적으로 상호작용하는 동물들은 포식자들이 잡기에 더 쉬울지도 모른다. 그러므로, 우리는 주의해야 하고 동물들을 위험에 빠뜨리지 않는 방식으로만 생태 관광을 활용해야 한다.

생태 관광은 사람들에게 환경을 존중하라고 가르치고, 일자리를 창출하며, 현지인들이 그들의 문화에 자부심을 느끼도록 돕는다.

UNIT 14 People

Reading 1

pp.60-61

Before Reading I think I would not be able to get my dream job and make money.

1 ④ **2** ④ **3** ③ **4** ④ **5** Strength, power, and courage were created by the Taliban's attack. **6** ②

해석

말랄라 유사프자이는 평화와 아동 인권의 세계적인 상징으로 알려져 있다. 말랄라가 11살이었을 때, 탈레반이 파키스탄에 있는 그녀의 마을을 장악했다. 여자아이들은 교육을 받는 것이 금지되었다. 학교에 다닐 수 없었기 때문에 말랄라는 대신 블로그에 글을 올렸다. (블로그는 방문객들이 의견을 남기고 메시지를 전송할 수 있게 해준다.) 그녀는 모든 사람이 교육을 받을 권리가 있다는 글을 썼다. 탈레반은 그녀를 멈추게 하고 싶어서 그녀를 죽이기 위해 누군가를 보냈다. 그 남자는 말랄라를 학교에 데려다주는 트럭에 탔고 총으로 그녀의 머리를 쐈다. 다행히도, 그녀는 살아남았다. 그리고 그녀는 그 공격이 그녀를 침묵하게 하는 것을 거부했다.

불과 9개월 후에, 그녀는 유엔에서 연설을 했다. 그녀는 "그들은 총알이 저를 침묵시킬 것이라고 생각했습니다. 하지만 그들은 실패했습니다. 그 침묵에서 수많은 목소리가 나왔습니다. 나약함, 두려움, 그리고 절망은 죽었습니다. 강인함, 힘, 그리고 용기가 태어났습니다."라고 말했다. 그녀의 말은 전 세계의 사람들에게 영감을 주었다. 2011년에, 그녀는 자신의 조국에서 청소년 평화상을 받았다. 그리고 2014년에, 그녀는 노벨 평화상을 받은 최연소 수상자가 되었다.

노벨 평화상 수상은 말랄라가 그녀의 노력을 계속할 수 있도록 용기를 주었다. "이 상은 그 목소리를 들어줘야 하는 모든 아이들을 위한 것입니다."라고 그녀는 말했다.

어휘

international ⑱국제적인, 세계적인   symbol ⑲상징(물)   peace ⑲평화   take over 장악하다   forbid ⑧금지하다   attend ⑧참석하다; *(~에) 다니다   comment ⑲의견, 논평   shoot ⑧(총 등을) 쏘다   survive ⑧살아남다   refuse ⑧거절하다, 거부하다   attack ⑲공격   silence ⑧침묵시키다 ⑲침묵   give a speech 연설하다 (speech ⑲연설)   bullet ⑲총알   fail ⑧실패하다   weakness ⑲나약함   fear ⑲두려움   hopelessness ⑲가망 없음, 절망   strength ⑲강인함, 힘   power ⑲*힘; 권력   courage ⑲용기   inspire ⑧고무하다; 영감을 주다   national ⑱국가의, 국가적인   prize ⑲상   encourage ⑧격려[고무]하다   effort ⑲노력   [문제] violence ⑲폭력   chore ⑲집안일   otherwise ⑨그렇지 않으면   fortunately ⑨다행스럽게도, 운 좋게도

8행   The man *got on* a truck [**that** was taking Malala to school] *and shot* her in the head.

- that: a truck을 수식하는 주격 관계대명사
- got on과 shot이 등위접속사 and로 연결된 병렬 구조

20행   Winning the Nobel Peace Prize **encouraged Malala to continue** her efforts.
주어   동사

- encourage + 목적어 + to-v: ~가 …하도록 격려하다

Reading 2   p.62

④

해석

최초의 국제 연합(UN) Youth Takeover가 2013년 7월 12일에 열렸다. 그 행사에는 전 세계에서 온 수백 명의 대표들이 있었지만, 세계의 주목을 받은 건 바로 말랄라의 연설이었다.

안녕하세요, 여러분. 제 이름은 말랄라이고, 저는 오늘 여러분과 이야기를 나눌 수 있게 된 것을 영광으로 생각합니다. 우리는 어둠을 볼 때, 빛의 중요성을 깨닫습니다. 우리가 침묵당할 때, 우리는 우리 목소리의 가치를 알게 됩니다. 저는 파키스탄에서 총에 맞닥뜨린 후에야 비로소 교육의 중요성을 깨달았습니다. 자신의 권리를 위해 투쟁하는 모든 여성과 아이는 책과 펜이라는 그들의 가장 강력한 무기를 들어야만 합니다. 한 명의 아이, 한 명의 선생님, 한 개의 펜, 그리고 한 권의 책이 함께 세상을 바꿀 수 있습니다.

어휘

take place 개최되다, 열리다   representative 圀 대표(자)   attention 圀 주의 (집중), 주목   honored 㔧 명예로운; *영광으로 생각하여   darkness 圀 어둠, 암흑   realize 㐐 깨닫다, 알아차리다   importance 圀 중요성   value 圀 가치   face 㐐 직면하다   struggle 㐐 투쟁하다   weapon 圀 무기   [문제] military 圀 군대   resource 圀 자원

구문 해설

2행   ..., but **it was** Malala's speech **that** got the world's attention.
- it is ~ that ...: …인 것은 바로 ~이다(강조구문)

6행   **It wasn't until** I was faced with guns in Pakistan **that** I realized the importance of education.
- it is not until ~ that ...: ~한 후에야 비로소 …하다

Unit Review

A `Reading 1` forbade, education, shot, survived, symbol

B **1** weapon **2** speech **3** refuse **4** struggle **5** international **6** weakness

Reading 1 해석

말랄라 유사프자이가 11살이었을 때, 탈레반이 그녀의 마을을 장악했다. 그들은 여자아이들이 학교에 가는 것을 금지했다. 그래서 말랄라는 대신 블로그에 글을 올렸다. 그녀는 모든 사람에게 교육을 받을 권리가 있다는 글을 썼다. 그러던 어느 날, 그녀는 탈레반의 조직원이 쏜 총에 맞았다. 다행히도, 그녀는 살아남았고, 그 이후에 국제 연합(UN)에서 감동적인 연설을 했다. 2014년에, 그녀는 노벨 평화상을 받은 최연소 수상자가 되었다. 이제 그녀는 평화와 아동 인권의 세계적인 상징이 되었다.

UNIT 15 *Technology*

Reading 1

pp.64-65

`Before Reading` Yes, I think all hackers are bad. They steal information from people.

1 ① **2** The idea for these terms comes from old Western movies in America. **3** ③
4 ④ **5** ③ **6** ④

해석

많은 사람들은 해커가 사이버 범죄자라고 생각한다. 이 사람들은 해커들이 그저 웹사이트와 컴퓨터 시스템에 침입하여, 이기적인 이유로 문제를 일으킨다고 생각한다. 이 해커들은 블랙 햇 해커라고 불린다. 그러나 해커의 유형은 하나 이상이다.

다른 해커들은 화이트 햇 해커라고 불린다. 이 해커들은 사람들을 돕는다. 이러한 용어들에 대한 아이디어는 미국의 오래된 서부 영화에서 유래한다. 이 영화들에서 영웅들은 항상 하얀 모자를 쓰고, 나쁜 사람들은 검은 모자를 쓴다. 같은 방식으로, 화이트 햇 해커는 피해를 방지하는 반면 블랙 햇 해커는 피해를 끼친다.

블랙 햇 해커들은 은행 계좌번호와 로그인 정보와 같은 중요한 정보를 사람들로부터 훔친다. 그리고 그들은 돈을 벌거나 사회에 문제를 일으키기 위해 그것을 사용한다. 화이트 햇 해커들은 블랙 햇 해커들과 같은 방법을 사용하지만, 그들은 그것을 할 수 있는 허가를 가지고 있다. 시스템에서 정보를 훔치는 대신, 그들은 그것의 보안상 약점을 찾는다. 그런 다음 그들은 (시스템의) 소유주가 그러한 약점을 고치도록 돕는다. 이러한 이유로, 이 해커들은 수요가 많다.

요즘, 사이버 범죄는 매우 흔해지고 있다. 그것이 화이트 햇 해커들이 중요한 이유이다. 그들은 중요한 정보를 보호하고 사람들을 온라인에서 안전하게 하는 것을 돕는다.

어휘

hacker 똉 해커 (hacking 똉 해킹)　cybercriminal 똉 사이버 범죄자 (cybercrime 똉 사이버 범죄)　break into 침입하다

selfish 형이기적인 hero 명영웅 harm 명해, 피해 steal 동훔치다 account 명계좌 detail 명세부 사항; *정보
society 명사회 method 명방법 permission 명허락, 허가 look for ~을 찾다 security 명보안 owner 명주인
in demand 수요가 많은 (demand 명요구, 수요) [문제] prevent 동막다, 방지하다 enter 동들어가다 direct 형직접적
인 opposite 형반대의

구문 해설

14행   White hat hackers use **the same** methods **as** black hat hackers, but they have permission [*to do* it].
   • the same A as B: B와 같은 A
   • to do: permission을 수식하는 형용사적 용법의 to부정사

16행   Then they **help the owners fix** those weaknesses.
   • help + 목적어 + (to) 동사원형: ~가 …하도록 돕다

19행   They **help protect** important information and *keep people safe* online.
   • help + (to) 동사원형: ~하도록 돕다, ~에 도움이 되다
   • keep + 목적어 + 형용사: ~을 …하게 유지하다

Reading 2   p.66

②

해석

해커들은 인터넷을 사용하는 사람들에게 지속적인 위협이다. 다행스럽게도, 당신이 해킹당할 가능성을 낮출 수 있는 쉬운 방법들이 있다. 우선, 피싱 이메일을 알아차리는 방법을 배워라. 만약 당신이 보낸 사람의 이메일 주소를 알지 못한다면, 그냥 그 이메일을 삭제하라. 그리고 절대로 거기에서 링크를 클릭하거나 프로그램을 다운로드 받지 마라. 둘째, 정기적으로 검색 기록을 삭제하라. 이것은 해커들이 당신의 온라인 생활에 대한 정보를 모으는 것을 방지한다. (당신의 온라인 생활은 당신이 매우 다양한 정보에 접근할 수 있게 한다.) 마지막으로, 당신의 컴퓨터 또는 기기가 필요하지 않을 때 전원을 꺼라. 당신이 온라인 상태가 아니면 해커들이 당신을 공격하기 더 어렵다. 이러한 간단한 조언들로, 당신은 온라인 위협을 방지하고 당신의 정보를 안전하게 지킬 수 있다.

어휘

constant 형지속적인 threat 명위협 thankfully 부고맙게도, 다행스럽게도 lower 동낮추다 chance 명가능성
hack 동해킹하다 first of all 우선 recognize 동알아보다, 알다 phishing 명피싱(전화·인터넷을 통한 신용 정보 노출 및 금융 사기 행위) delete 동삭제하다 search history 검색 기록 regularly 부정기[규칙]적으로 gather 동모으다
enable 동~을 할 수 있게 하다 access 동접근하다 a wide variety of 매우 다양한 device 명장치, 기구 target 동
목표[표적]로 삼다, 겨냥하다 tip 명조언 avoid 동피하다; 방지하다

구문 해설

1행   Thankfully, there are easy ways [**to lower** your chances of *being hacked*].

- to lower: easy ways를 수식하는 형용사적 용법의 to부정사로 '~하는'의 의미
- being hacked: 전치사 of의 목적어로 쓰인 동명사구

8행   It's harder <u>for hackers</u> <u>to target you</u> if you aren't online.
            가주어   의미상 주어   진주어

Unit Review   p.67

A   [Reading 1] enter, selfish, safe, weaknesses   [Reading 2] deleting

B   **1** threat   **2** permission   **3** constant   **4** hero   **5** lower   **6** selfish

---

Reading 2 해석

피싱 이메일을 식별하는 방법을 배우고, 당신의 검색 기록을 정기적으로 <u>삭제하며</u>, 당신이 필요하지 않을 때 장치를 끔으로써 당신은 해킹당할 가능성을 제한할 수 있다.

UNIT 16 Entertainment

Reading 1   pp.68-69

[Before Reading] I haven't ever imagined vegetable instruments! But maybe carrots or pumpkins can be used as instruments.

1 ④   **2** ④   **3** ②   **4** ①   **5** they're waiting for some vegetable soup (that is made from the instruments)   **6** ④

해석

당근, 피망, 호박—대부분의 사람들은 이 채소들을 이용하여 저녁식사를 만든다. 그러나 비엔나 채소 오케스트라(Vienna Vegetable Orchestra)에게 그것들은 음악을 연주하기 위한 완벽한 악기이다! 1998년부터, 13명의 남녀로 이루어진 이 그룹은 채소로 음악을 만들어 전 세계에서 콘서트를 열어 오고 있다.

콘서트 날이다. 연주자들은 현지의 시장에 있다. 그들은 구입할 좋고 신선한 '악기'를 찾고 있다. 쇼핑 후에 그들은 악기를 만들기 시작한다. (신선한 채소는 건강한 식단의 중요한 부분이다.) 오로지 칼, 드릴과 상상력만으로 금세 당근 플루트, 피망 트럼펫과 호박 드럼이 만들어질 것이다! 이제 연주 시간이다. 콘서트가 시작되고 청중은 놀란다. 어떻게 채소가 그렇게 잔잔하고 위안이 되는 소리를 만들어 낼 수 있는 걸까? 그것은 다른 어떤 악기들도 만들어 낼 수 없는 독특한 소리이다. 게다가, 채소의 신선한 냄새가 콘서트홀 전체를 채운다.

공연이 끝나더라도 아무도 콘서트홀을 떠나지 않는다. 왜일까? 그들은 그 악기들로 만들어진 채소 수프를 기다리고 있다! 이 특별한 오케스트라는 당신의 귀뿐만 아니라 당신의 코와 배도 즐겁게 해준다.

pepper 명후추; *피망   vegetable 명채소   instrument 명악기   musician 명음악가, 연주자   healthy 형건강한
diet 명식단   drill 명송곳, 드릴   imagination 명상상력   audience 명청중   calm 형고요한, 평온한   comforting
형위안을 주는   unique 형독특한   in addition 게다가   fill 동채우다   whole 형전체의, 모든   performance 명공연
be over 끝나다   wait for ~을 기다리다   please 동즐겁게 하다

구문 해설

4행   ... this group of thirteen men and women **has been** ⎡ **making** music with vegetables
and
⎣ **giving** concerts around the world.

13행   How can the vegetables produce **such a calm and comforting sound**?
• such + 관사(a/an) + 형용사 + 명사: 그렇게 ~한 …

14행   It's a unique sound [**that** no other instruments can make].
• that: 선행사 a unique sound를 수식하는 절을 이끄는 목적격 관계대명사

Reading 2   p.70

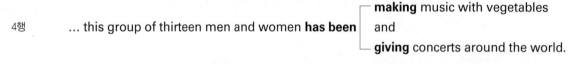

④

해석

비엔나 채소 오케스트라의 한 단원과의 인터뷰

Q 채소를 악기로 사용하는 이유가 무엇인가요?
A 채소는 아주 좋은 소리가 나는 데다 여러분은 냄새를 맡을 수도 있고 맛을 볼 수도 있습니다. 그리고 그것들은 서로 다른 많은 색깔과 모양이 있어 보기에도 좋습니다. 가장 중요한 것은 그것들을 어디서나 구할 수 있다는 것이지요.
Q 단원 모두가 채식주의자이신가요?
A 오, 저희는 그 질문을 너무 자주 들어요! 아뇨, 그렇지 않아요.
Q 콘서트를 준비하는 게 어려운가요?
A 가끔 적당한 채소를 찾는 것이 어렵습니다. 예를 들어, 당근 리코더를 만들기 위해서는 특별한 종류의 당근이 필요합니다. 어떤 나라에서는 (그것을) 구하기 어려울 수 있습니다.
Q 어떻게 모든 단원들이 같이 일할 수 있죠?
A 저희는 13명으로 음악에 대해 모두 다른 생각을 갖고 있어요. 그래서 저희는 연습 중에 많이 대화합니다. 이러한 방식으로 저희는 서로의 생각을 존중합니다.

어휘

taste 동맛보다   shape 명모양   vegetarian 명채식주의자   prepare 동준비하다   recorder 명리코더   practice 명
연습   respect 동존중하다   [문제] organize 동조직하다, 구성하다

2행	They're nice [**to look at**] too, *with* many different colors and shapes.

- to look at: 형용사 nice를 수식하는 부사적 용법의 to부정사로 '~하기에'의 의미
- with: ((소유)) ~으로, ~을 갖고

8행	Sometimes **it's** hard **to find** the right vegetables.

- it은 가주어이고, to find 이하는 진주어로 '~하는 것'의 의미

Unit Review

p.71

A [Reading 1] concerts, instruments, markets, soup

B **1** fill **2** please **3** diet **4** audience **5** shape **6** calm

Reading 1 해석

비엔나 채소 오케스트라는 콘서트를 열며 전 세계를 순회한다. 그 오케스트라의 모든 악기들이 채소들로 만들어지기 때문에 매우 특별하다. 단원들은 매 콘서트 당일에 현지의 시장에서 채소들을 산다. 그러고 나서 그들은 그것들을 악기로 만든다. 음악은 차분하고 편하며, 채소들은 아주 좋은 향이 난다. 콘서트가 끝나면, 그 악기들은 채소 수프로 만들어지는데, 이 수프는 청중과 함께 나눠 먹는다.

UNIT 17 The Arts

Reading 1

pp.72-73

[Before Reading] The paintings look colorful. It seems that they drew people in a kind of a strange way.

1 ② **2** Egyptian painters followed the same rules for more than 3,500 years **3** ③
4 ① **5** ④ **6** (1) F (2) T

해석

고대 이집트를 생각할 때 우리는 거대한 피라미드를 상상한다. 그러나 고대 이집트인들은 그림을 포함하여 많은 종류의 예술품 또한 만들었다. 이집트 화가들은 똑같은 규칙들을 3,500년이 넘도록 따랐다! 그래서 고대 이집트 양식을 알아보는 것은 쉽다.

이집트 화가들은 사람들을 자주 그렸다. 그러나 그들이 그린 사람들은 별로 사실적으로 보이지 않았다. 만일 당신이 그들처럼 서 있으려 한다면 당신은 넘어질 것이다! 화가들은 신체의 각 부분을 그것이 가장 좋게 보이는 각도에서 그렸다. 머리는 코와 입의 모양이 보일 수 있도록 측면에서 (본 모양으로) 그려졌다. 그러나 눈은 정면에서 (본 모양으로) 그려졌는데 그런 식으로 해야 그것이 가장 흥미롭게 보였기 때문이다. 상체 또한 정면에서 (본 모양으로) 그려졌다. 그러나 다리는 그 사람이 걷고 있는 것처럼 측면에서 (본 모양으로)

그려졌다.

사람의 크기에 대한 규칙들도 있었다. 크기는 그 사람이 얼마나 중요한지를 보여 주는 데 사용되었다. 물론 왕들은 그림에서 매우 큰 모습으로 등장했다. 그러나 신들이 그려질 때 그들의 크기는 훨씬 더 컸다.

이제, 이러한 규칙들을 염두에 둔다면 이집트 그림들이 보기에 더 재미있을 것이다.

어휘

think of ~을 생각하다   ancient 형고대의   Egyptian 명이집트인 형이집트의   including 전~을 포함하여   follow 동 따르다   rule 명규칙   fall over 넘어지다   draw 동(선을 이용하여) 그리다   angle 명각도   side 명옆(면), 측면   front 명정면, 앞   upper 형위쪽의   appear 동나타나다   [문제] realistic 형사실적인   describe 동묘사하다   various 형다 양한   be interested in ~에 관심이 있다

구문 해설

6행   However, the people [(that) they painted] didn't **look** very **realistic**.

- the people 뒤에는 목적격 관계대명사 that 또는 whom이 생략되어 있음
- look + 형용사: ~하게 보이다

14행   Size **was used to show** *how important the person was.*

- be used to-v: ~하는 데 쓰이다
- how 이하는 show의 목적어 역할을 하는 간접의문문

17행   Now, **with** these rules **in mind**, Egyptian paintings *should* be more interesting to look at.

- with ~ in mind: ~을 염두에 두고
- should: '~일 것이다'라는 기대·가정의 의미로 사용된 조동사

Reading 2   p.74

⑤

해석

이집트 그림에서는 색들이 아주 중요했다. 화가들은 오직 여섯 개의 색들만 사용했다. 이 색들은 특별한 의미를 지녔다. 빨강은 권력 과 불의 색이었다. 초록은 자연과 새로운 생명을 나타냈다. 파랑은 하늘과 상상력의 색이었다. 노랑은 태양과 장수를 위한 것이었다. 흰 색은 순수한 아름다움을 나타냈고, 검은색은 죽음을 나타냈다. 화가들은 항상 신들과 여신들을 특정한 색깔로 그렸다. 예를 들어 식 물과 탄생의 신인 오시리스는 항상 초록색으로 그려졌다. 하늘의 여신인 누트는 언제나 파란색으로 그려졌다.

어휘

artist 명화가, 예술가   pure 형순수한   goddess 명여신   certain 형일정한, 특정한

5행 Artists always **painted** <u>gods and goddesses</u> <u>certain colors</u>.
　　　　　　　　　　　목적어　　　　　　　　목적보어

• paint + 목적어 + 목적보어: ~을 …으로 칠하다

Unit Review   p.75

A Reading 1 recognize, angles, front, Size, Gods

B **1** upper **2** follow **3** side **4** angle **5** pure **6** ancient

UNIT 18 Sports

Reading 1   pp.76-77

Before Reading I haven't tried chess, but I'd love to learn how to play. I don't know how to box either.

1 ① **2** ③ **3** ③ **4** ② **5** ② **6** switching between strength exercises and speed chess games

해석

종이 울리고 두 명의 강한 선수들이 복싱 링 안으로 걸어들어 간다. 여러분은 다음에 무슨 일이 일어날지 알아맞힐 수 있는가? 그들은 테이블에 앉아서 체스를 두기 시작한다! 이것은 체스복싱이라고 불리는 인기 있는 새로운 스포츠에서 일어나는 일이다.

체스복싱 경기 초반에, 선수들은 4분 동안 체스를 둔다. 그러고 나서, 그들은 자신의 코너로 가서 복싱 글러브를 낀다. 체스판이 치워지고 나면, 3분간의 복싱 경기가 시작된다. (고대 그리스인들은 신들이 복싱을 즐겨 했다고 생각해서, 복싱은 기원전 688년 즈음 올림픽 경기의 일부가 되었다.) 선수들은 11라운드까지 체스와 복싱을 계속해서 번갈아 한다. 경기는 선수들 중 한 명이 쓰러지면 끝난다. 또한 선수 한 명이 체스에서 지거나 체스를 두는 동안 시간을 다 쓰면 경기가 끝난다.

최초의 체스복싱 대회는 2003년 독일에서 개최되었다. 그 이후로, 이 스포츠는 전 세계에 있는 나라들로 확산되어 왔다. 선수들은 (서로) 다른 방식으로 체스복싱 대회를 준비한다. 자주 사용되는 한 가지 방법은 근력 운동과 스피드 체스 경기를 번갈아가며 하는 것이다. 이것은 선수들이 실제 시합의 특이한 리듬에 익숙해지도록 돕는다!

어휘

ring ⑲링, 원형 경기장 ⑧(종 등이) 울리다　boxing ⑲권투, 복싱 (box ⑧권투를 하다)　match ⑲경기, 시합　chessboard ⑲체스판　take away 제거하다, 치우다　round ⑲회[라운드]　continue ⑧계속하다　switch ⑧전환하다, 바꾸다　knock out ~을 나가 떨어지게 하다, ~을 의식을 잃게 만들다　run out of ~을 다 써버리다　competition ⑲경쟁; *대회, 시합

37

spread ⑧퍼지다, 확산되다   strength exercise 근력 운동 (strength ⑲힘, 기운)   unusual ⑲특이한, 흔치 않은   real ⑲진짜의, 실제의   [문제] champion ⑲챔피언, 우승자   rare ⑲드문, 희귀한

구문 해설

3행   This is **what** happens in a popular new sport [(which is) called chess boxing].

- what: 선행사를 포함하는 관계대명사로 '~하는 것'의 의미
- sport 뒤에는 '주격 관계대명사 + be동사'가 생략되어 있음

14행   Since then, the sport **has spread** to countries all over the world.
- has spread: 계속의 현재완료 시제로 '~해 오고 있다'의 의미

17행   This **helps the fighters** *get* used to the unusual rhythm of a real match!
- help + 목적어 + 동사원형: ~가 …하도록 돕다
- get used to + (동)명사: ~에 익숙해지다

Reading 2   p.78

④

해석

체스복싱에 대한 발상은 원래 프랑스 만화가인 Enki Bilal의 1992년 그래픽 노벨인 'Froid Équateur'에서 비롯되었다. 하지만 네덜란드 예술가인 Iepe Rubingh은 이러한 발상을 현실로 바꾸었다. Bilal의 그래픽 노벨에서는 전체 복싱 경기가 개최되고 나서 체스 경기가 이어진다. Rubingh은 선수들이 체스 경기와 복싱을 번갈아가며 하도록 규칙들을 변경했다.

시간이 지나면서, 점점 더 많은 사람들이 체스복싱에 관심을 갖게 되었다. 현재 대회들은 유럽, 미국, 그리고 일본에서 개최된다. 아마도 머지않아 여러분 가까이에 체스복싱 시합이 생길 것이다!

어휘

originally ⑨원래, 본래   French ⑲프랑스의, 프랑스인[어]의   cartoonist ⑲만화가   Dutch ⑲네덜란드의, 네덜란드인[어]의   reality ⑲현실

구문 해설

2행   But the Dutch artist Iepe Rubingh **turned** this idea **into** a reality.
- turn A into B: A를 B로 바꾸다

4행   Rubingh changed the rules **so that** fighters switch between rounds of chess and boxing.
- so that ~: (목적의 부사절을 이끌어) ~하기 위하여, ~이 되도록

A Reading 1 switch, knocked, prepare, strength   Reading 2 reality

B **1** originally **2** take away **3** spread **4** match **5** continue **6** switch

Reading 1 해석

체스복싱이라고 불리는 인기 있는 새로운 스포츠에서, 선수들은 11라운드까지 체스 경기와 복싱을 번갈아 한다. 선수들 중 한 명이 쓰러지거나 체스 경기에서 지면, 시합은 끝난다. 최초의 체스복싱 대회는 2003년 독일에서 개최되었다. 이제 대회는 전 세계에서 열린다. 선수들은 보통 근력 운동과 스피드 체스 경기를 번갈아 함으로써 체스복싱 대회를 준비한다. 이것은 그들이 체스복싱의 특이한 리듬에 익숙해지도록 해준다.

Reading 2 해석

체스복싱은 프랑스 만화가 Enki Bilal에 의해 발명되었고, 네덜란드 예술가 Iepe Rubingh이 그것을 현실로 만든 이후 인기를 끌었다.

UNIT 19 *Origins*

Reading 1   pp.80-81

Before Reading I don't know exactly when. I guess the history of T-shirts may not be that long.

1 ② **2** ④ **3** ② **4** ② **5** share their likes and dislikes **6** (1) T (2) F

해석

티셔츠 없는 삶을 상상하기란 어렵다. 그러나 티셔츠는 1960년대가 되어서야 비로소 인기를 끌게 되었다.

제1차 세계 대전 중에 미국 군인들은 유럽의 무더운 여름에 모직 유니폼을 입었다. 그들은 유럽 군인들이 면 속셔츠를 입고 있는 것을 보았고 그들의 스타일을 모방하기 시작했다. 그것은 그 단순한 모양 때문에 티셔츠(T-shirts)라고 불렸다. 제2차 세계 대전 무렵에 이르러 미국의 육군과 해군 모두는 그것을 그들의 유니폼에 포함시켰다.

1950년대까지도 티셔츠는 여전히 속옷으로 여겨졌다. 영화에서 그것을 입음으로써 청중에게 충격을 준 것은 바로 배우 말론 브란도와 제임스 딘이었다. 사람들은 스크린에서 속옷을 겉옷으로 입은 것을 보고 놀랐다. 제임스 딘은 그것을 그의 영화 '이유 없는 반항'에서 입었을 때 티셔츠를 멋진 젊은이의 상징으로 만들었다. 그리고 그의 몸을 드러낸 딱 붙는 스타일은 금세 인기를 끌었다.

1960년대 인쇄술의 발달은 티셔츠에 또 다른 변화를 가져왔다. 바로 사람들이 티셔츠에 인쇄를 하기 시작한 것이다. 이 저렴한 면 캔버스는 입는 사람들이 그들의 좋고 싫음을 공유하는 한 방법이 되었다. 그 이후로 티셔츠는 훨씬 더 인기를 누리게 되었다. 왜 안 그렇겠는가? 그것은 비싸지 않고, 편안하고, 멋지고, 재미있기까지 하니 말이다!

wool ⑲양모; *직물 uniform ⑲제복, 군복 cotton ⑲면 undershirt ⑲속셔츠 copy ⑧모방하다, 복사하다
army ⑲군대; *육군 navy ⑲해군 include ⑧포함하다 consider ⑧여기다, 생각하다 underwear ⑲내의, 속옷
shock ⑧충격을 주다 outerwear ⑲겉옷 symbol ⑲상징 youth ⑲젊음; 젊은이 rebel ⑲반항 cause ⑲이유, 원
인 tight ⑲딱 붙는 development ⑲발달 printing ⑲인쇄(술) inexpensive ⑲비싸지 않은 canvas ⑲캔버스 천,
화폭 share ⑧공유하다 comfortable ⑲편안한 stylish ⑲멋진 [문제] memory ⑲기억

구문 해설

4행 They ┌ **saw European soldiers wearing** cotton undershirts
           │ and
           └ *started copying* their style.

- 지각동사(see) + 목적어 + v-ing: ~가 …하고 있는 것을 보다
- start v-ing: ~하기 시작하다 (start는 to부정사와 동명사 모두를 목적어로 취할 수 있음)

10행 **It was** actors Marlon Brando and James Dean **who** shocked audiences *by wearing* them in movies.

- it is ~ that[who] ...: …한 것[사람]은 바로 ~이다 (강조구문)
- by v-ing: ~함으로써

16행 ... became a way **for wearers** [*to share* their likes and dislikes].

- for wearers: to share의 의미상 주어
- to share: '~하는'의 의미로 a way를 수식하는 형용사적 용법의 to부정사

Reading 2   p.82

④

해석

폴로 셔츠로도 알려진 테니스 셔츠는 깃이 있는 두꺼운 면 티셔츠이다. 그것은 1926년에 프랑스의 테니스 챔피언인 René Lacoste에 의해 발명되었다. **(C)** 그 당시 테니스 선수들은 대체로 긴 소매 셔츠를 입고 타이를 맸다. Lacoste는 그것들이 너무 덥고 불편하다고 생각했다. 그래서 그는 새로운 테니스 셔츠를 디자인했고 그것을 한 경기에서 입었다. **(A)** 곧 그의 새 디자인은 다른 테니스 선수들 사이에서 인기를 끌게 되었다. 1930년대에는 심지어 폴로 선수들도 그것을 그들의 유니폼의 일부로 입기 시작했다. **(B)** 오늘날 이 테니스 셔츠, 혹은 폴로 셔츠는 스포츠 선수들만을 위한 것이 아니다. 그것은 모든 사람의 일상 패션이 되었다.

thick 형두꺼운   collar 명깃, 칼라   invent 동발명하다   long-sleeved 형긴 소매의   uncomfortable 형불편한

구문 해설

3행   In the 1930s, even polo players **began to wear** it *as* parts of their uniform.
 • begin to-v: ~하기 시작하다 (begin은 to부정사와 동명사 모두를 목적어로 취할 수 있음)
 • as: 《자격》 ~로(서)

Unit Review   p.83

A   [Reading 1] soldiers, outerwear, print, showing   [Reading 2] uncomfortable

B   **1** tight   **2** share   **3** thick   **4** youth   **5** comfortable   **6** copy

Reading 2 해석

René Lacoste는 긴 소매 셔츠와 타이가 너무 <u>불편했기</u> 때문에 폴로 셔츠를 발명했고, 이 셔츠는 이후 모두를 위한 일상적인 패션 아이템이 되었다.

UNIT *20* *Space*

Reading 1   pp.84-85

[Before Reading] I've seen them wearing special spacesuits on TV.

1 ②   **2** build or fix things on it   **3** ③   **4** ③   **5** ②   **6** (1) F (2) T

해석

당신은 아마도 우주 비행사들이 우주선 밖에서 일하는 것을 TV로 본 적이 있을 것이다. 이것은 우주 유영이라고 불린다. 우주 비행사들은 그들의 우주선에 있는 것들을 조립하거나 고치기 위해 우주 유영을 한다. 그들은 우주 유영 중 우주복을 입는데, 우주 유영은 8시간까지 길어질 수도 있다. 그리고 이 우주복은 단순한 옷 그 이상이다.

우주복은 개인용 우주선과도 같다. 그것은 서로 다른 많은 부분들로 이루어져 있으며 각 부분은 우주 비행사를 우주에서 안전하게 지켜 준다. 예를 들어, 우주복 뒤에 있는 배낭에는 우주 비행사가 숨 쉴 수 있는 산소가 들어있다. 이것은 또한 마실 수 있는 물통도 있다. 우주복 자체의 내부에도 물이 있다. 그 물은 우주 비행사의 속옷 속에 있는 관들을 통해 흐른다. 이것은 우주에서 그들을 시원하게 유지해준다. 우주복에 있는 작은 분사 추진기들 또한 우주 비행사를 안전하게 하는 것을 돕는다. 이것은 우주 비행사가 우주선에서 멀리 떨어진 곳으로 떠다니게 될 경우 다시 날아서 돌아갈 수 있도록 돕는다. (그리고 우주 먼지는 우주 유영을 힘들게 만든다.) 물론 우

주 비행사들이 우주에서 일하게 하는 것을 가능하게 해주는 무전기, 배터리, 컴퓨터 같은 시스템들도 있다.

이 모든 부분들을 고려할 때 우주복이 약 280킬로그램의 무게가 나가는 것은 놀라운 일이 아니다. 그러나 우주의 무중력 덕분에 우주 비행사들은 이 무거운 옷을 입고서도 엄청난 일을 할 수 있다.

어휘

astronaut 명우주 비행사   spacecraft 명우주선   spacewalk 명우주 유영   fix 동고치다   spacesuit 명우주복   be made up of ~으로 이루어지다   space 명공간; *우주   backpack 명배낭   suit 명(복장의) 한 벌, 옷   contain 동~이 들어있다   oxygen 명산소   breathe 동숨 쉬다   flow 동흐르다   tube 명관   jet 명분출; 제트기, 분사 추진기   float 동뜨다   dust 명먼지   radio 명무전기   considering 전~을 고려하면   weigh 동~의 무게가 나가다   weightlessness 명무중력 (상태) (weight 명무게)   [문제] feature 명특징, 특색; 기능   personal 형개인적인   hold 동수용하다   a couple of 둘의, (몇)개의

구문 해설

7행   It is made up of many different parts, and each part **keeps the astronaut safe** in space.
- keep + 목적어 + 형용사: ~을 …하게 유지하다

15행   ... systems [**like** a radio, a battery, and a computer] [to *let the astronaut work* in space].
- like: 《전치사》~ 같은
- 사역동사(let) + 목적어 + 동사원형: ~이 …하게 하다

17행   Considering all the parts, **it's not surprising that** a spacesuit weighs about 280 kg.
- it's not surprising that ~: ~은 놀랄 일이 아니다 (it은 가주어, that 이하는 진주어임)

Reading 2   p.86

①

해석

우주 유영을 가기 전 우주 비행사들은 우주복 그 이상을 필요로 한다. 즉, 많은 훈련이 필요하다. 이곳 지구에는 우주 비행사들이 우주 유영을 준비하도록 돕는 많은 트레이너들이 있다.

로스: 저는 우주 비행사들이 우주복을 정확히 입도록 훈련시킵니다. 우주복은 많은 부분들로 이루어져 있기 때문에, 우주복을 입는 데에 약 45분이 걸립니다. 저는 또한 그들에게 우주복 안에 있는 다른 도구들을 사용하는 방법을 가르칩니다.

유민: 저는 우주 비행사들에게 우주 유영에 대한 모든 것을 가르칩니다. 우선, 저는 그들에게 특수한 수중 방에서 무중력 상태에 있도록 훈련시킵니다. 그런 다음 그들에게 우주선 밖에서 일을 하는 방법을 보여 줍니다. 제 일은 매우 중요합니다.

팀: 제 업무는 우리가 우주 비행사들을 훈련시키기 위해 사용하는 기술을 관리하는 것입니다. 우주 비행사들은 컴퓨터 화면이 있는 특수 헬멧을 씁니다. 이것은 그들에게 우주 유영이 어떤 것인지를 '보게' 해줍니다. 우주 비행사들은 이 부분의 훈련을 매우 즐깁니다!

train ⑧훈련시키다 (trainer ⑲훈련자, 트레이너) put on ∼을 입다 tool ⑲도구 underwater ⑲수중의 manage ⑧ 관리하다 technology ⑲과학 기술 [문제] escape ⑲탈출 spaceship ⑲우주선

구문 해설

4행 Because it is made up of many parts, **putting on a spacesuit** *takes* about 45 minutes.
- putting on a spacesuit는 주어로 사용된 동명사구로, 단수 취급하므로 동사는 takes임
- take + 시간: ∼의 시간이 걸리다

10행 My job is **managing** the technology [(that) we use *to train* astronauts].
- managing: is의 보어로 사용된 동명사로 '∼하는 것'의 의미
- the technology 뒤에는 목적격 관계대명사 which 또는 that이 생략됨
- to train: 목적을 나타내는 부사적 용법의 to부정사

11행 These **allow them to "see"** *what a spacewalk is like*.
- allow + 목적어 + to-v: ∼가 …하는 것을 허락하다
- what 이하는 see의 목적어 역할을 하는 간접의문문이며 'what ∼ like'는 '∼가 어떠한지'로 해석함

Unit Review p.87

A Reading 1 safe, spacewalks, oxygen, jets

B 1 astronaut 2 tool 3 float 4 breathe 5 dust 6 fix

Reading 1 해석

우주복은 우주 비행사의 가장 중요한 장비의 부품이다. 그것은 우주 비행사가 우주선 밖에서 일하고 있는 동안 우주 비행사를 안전하게 지켜준다. 우주 비행사들은 또한 때때로 우주 유영을 할 필요가 있다. 우주복이 없다면 이것은 불가능할 것이다. 산소가 들어있는 배낭과 물 가방과 같은 특별한 장치들은 우주 비행사들이 호흡하고 수분을 유지하게 한다. 우주복에는 또한 여러 분사 추진기가 있는데, 이것은 우주 비행사들이 우주선으로 돌아오는 것을 돕는다.

MEMO

MEMO

MEMO

MEMO

JUNIOR
READING EXPERT

Level **2**